C000091044

As Man and Woman Made

Theological Reflections on Marriage

Edited by Susan Durber

As Man and Woman Made

Theological Reflections on Marriage

Edited by Susan Durber

ISBN 0 85346 139 2
Published by the United Reformed Church
86 Tavistock Place, London WC1H 9RT

© The United Reformed Church 1994
except for contributions by
Janet Elizabeth Chesney, Colin Gunton and Jean Mortimer.
Cover © 'Hugging Couple' by Lynne Gant, illustrator

Biblical quotations are from the New Revised Standard Version,
unless otherwise stated.

All rights reserved. No part of this publication may be reproduced,
stored in a retrieval system, or transmitted in any form, electronic,
mechanical, photocopying, recording, or other means without the
prior permission of the publisher.

Printed by Witney Press Ltd

to Michael

Contents

Contributors List

Janet Elizabeth Chesney is Principal of a school in New Zealand.

Ruth Clarke is a URC member.

David Cockerell is Adult Education and Training Officer for the Diocese of Ely.

Graham Cook is Director of the Windermere Centre.

Martin Cressey is Principal of Westminster College, Cambridge.

Susan Durber is the minister of Salford Central United Reformed Church and a tutor at the Northern Baptist College.

Colin Gunton is Professor of Christian Doctrine at King's College, London.

Brian Haymes is President of Bristol Baptist College.

David Hilborn is the minister of The City Temple, London.

Elizabeth King is minister of Temple Cowley United Reformed Church, Oxford.

Jean Mortimer is a URC minister.

Margaret Nuttall is Chaplain at St Peter's Hospice, Bristol.

Peter Rand is minister within the Darwen Group of United Reformed Churches and a member of the Blackburn RELATE group.

Elizabeth Stuart is a lecturer at The College of St Mark and St John, Plymouth and author of *Daring to Speak Love's Name,* Hamish Hamilton, 1993.

John Taylor is a retired URC minister.

Elizabeth Templeton is a member of the Church of Scotland and a freelance theologian and writer.

David Thompson is a Fellow of Fitzwilliam College Cambridge and the convenor of the URC's Doctrine and Worship Committee.

Bernard Thorogood was formerly General Secretary of the United Reformed Church and is now a minister of the Uniting Church in Australia in retirement.

Janet Wootton is minister of Union Chapel, Islington.

Frances Young is Edward Cadbury Professor at the University of Birmingham.

Introduction

Susan Durber

I have been reflecting on my own embarrassment at having been
asked to edit a book on marriage and theology. Marriage seems,
as the Church does sometimes, to be a dying institution, a leftover
from another age. In the kind of circles in which I often move, we talk
of our 'partners' rather than of our husbands and wives and we
grimace as we look at our wedding photos - if we have them.
Marriage isn't 'right on' anymore. Few of my friends, within or
without the church, would defend anymore the Church's perceived
teaching: 'Celibacy before marriage and chastity within it' - at least
in its most obvious sense. Neither would we want to talk about
relationships in a way which excludes others or privileges one
particular way of sustaining love.

However, perhaps because I find embarrassment such an uncomfortable thing, I agreed to work at the issues by working on this book.
I value enormously my own marriage relationship and believe it to
have been a place in which I have known the love and grace of God.
I want to be able to talk about marriage, and my marriage, within the
context of faith, but in ways which do not threaten the well-being of
others or contradict my own deep concerns for justice and freedom for
all people. I want to be able to talk theological words (if I cannot
make theological sense) as I reflect on my living of a particular way
of loving within a very plural culture and within a particular stream of
religious tradition. As I searched the shelves for books on theology
and marriage, my embarrassment deepened. There were yards of
books from fundamentalist Protestant traditions and several inches
from Roman Catholics and Anglicans, all with their own particular
agenda and concerns. There didn't seem to be many books at all
by people who shared my sense of embarrassment or who were asking
my sorts of questions. I recognise that I may not have looked hard
enough, but this book is the result of my dismay before the book-
shelves. I have prepared this book as part of my work as a member of
the URC's 'Doctrine and Worship Committee' who shared my dismay,
though not all the members would share my particular perspective! In
bringing these chapters together, I have stirred into speech the kinds of
voices which have often been silent (or even silenced) on the subject
of marriage and those things that go with it. I hope that the resulting
conversation will prove to be of value. For too long, the voices of
reform/Reform have been too quiet though other, to me more

7

ominous, sounds have been heard. I would be glad to know that this was but one stage of what should be a long and intense discussion.

This book has brought together different theological methods and stances to create what, I hope, will be a useful resource. It has been said that texts or books can speak to one another as they stand side by side on the shelf. Between these covers the different chapters, styles and methods may well argue with one another and will find no simple agreement, but their encounters with one another should be eventful. Here are texts that begin with history, sacred text and tradition. But here are also texts which begin the theological task rooted in experience. Here are texts which stand steadfastly in the stream of Christian inheritance and tradition. Here also are texts which take very seriously their position within a contemporary culture in which much is being challenged and overturned. Conservatism and radicalism, reform and revolution are all here. If the authors of these texts were gathered around a dinner table, the talk would be intense and sometimes fraught. As these texts are gathered between the same covers, the intertextuality should create sparks. The book does not toe a consistent line, but reflects the plural community in which we all, in a sense, now participate. However, I hope that no reader could escape without facing the challenge of the need to think about marriage and theology in new ways - ways which are true both to our times and to our tradition.

The chapters are held together in sections by phrases taken from the marriage service in the URC Service Book (1989). In these sections small conversations may take place within the larger discussion. What does Elizabeth Stuart's 'theology of friendship' say to David Hilborn's chapter on the 'procreation of children', for example? More broadly, what does Elizabeth Templeton's suggestion that marriage may be 'sinful' in its exclusivism say to the very many affirmations of the value of fidelity to one partner found in this book? How does the feminist critique talk with the strong themes of God's involvement in marriage? There are many fruitful potential conversations here and not just the ones I have arranged. All the chapters also engage with other texts written on this same subject - and there have been many in Christian tradition. I hope that they will move the conversation on.

The book could, of course, simply be read from cover to cover. I hope too that it may provide some fruitful material for discussion groups so that the conversation will continue in other places and in other contexts. For too long, we have kept silence when we should have spoken.

Towards a theology of marriage

Elizabeth Templeton

Marriage, I suppose, deserves a theology as much as other things. If one can have a theology of work, of leisure, of desire, of sport, of public life, of family, of sexuality, of co-existence, then marriage can claim a similar theological attention.

But that is not how the theology of marriage is usually addressed within churches. Rather it is seen as a privileged subject for theological reflection, one intimate to the very nature of theology, i.e. to discourse about God's self-disclosure to human beings. It is tied in with doctrines which are central to Christian self-understanding; creation, providence, ecclesiology and redemption.

In most churches within the North-Western world, (if one starts from a Eurocentric geography) marriage is seen as being at some sort of crisis point. Secular magazines and media discussions recurrently ask whether marriage and the nuclear family are obsolete institutions. Report after report is commissioned by anxious synods and assemblies, who find, or think they find, a widening gap between official church teaching and common practice. And the most alarming aspect of the situation to many is that the gap no longer coincides with the supposed fault-line between church and world. Christians are, on the whole, having sexual intercourse before marriage. (The recent survey of British sexual behaviour suggests that only one percent of those who marry are virgins, and the Christian population is therefore, in some measure, part of the ninety-nine percent who aren't.) Christians are increasingly finding the courage, much in debt to their secular peers, to say that they are gay or lesbian, and believe their relationships of dedicated love are God-given and God-affirmed. Christian feminists, as well as others, document the negativities of marriage as a relational structure, at least as commonly practised in our cultural history.

For some Christians this generates huge alarm. They find in such trends a sign of the widespread betrayal of God-given standards, a capitulation to the Zeitgeist and a loss of distinctive Christian identity. They believe that it is vital for the well-being of the Christian community, for society's health at large, and for the

9

integrity of the Gospel message, that standards which belong to the foundation-patterns of creation, and to the communities of God's salvation are not compromised.

For other Christians, and for the majority of outside observers, traditional church pronouncements in the area of sexual ethics are past their sell-by date, and the fact that the churches are beginning to acknowledge the complexity of their own social reality is a small sign of hope. Or it could be, if it can be given space to breathe and name itself within the Christian community as a whole, and not be driven underground by reactive denunciation.

My own theological reflections in this area have been tugged, so to speak, by two polar influences. One has been the critique of marriage as an essentially heterosexist and culturally constructed institution, a critique most forcefully voiced by my gay and lesbian friends, whose sensibility to church pronouncements on normative sexual mores has all the bite of famine victims talking about British Development Aid! The other has been my attempt to handle, within various ecclesiastical contexts, the fear and resistance there is to open discussion of these issues, and the common note of hysteria which characterises actual debate.

At the same time, I recognise myself as *partie prise* as a member of what is called in the Jargon "a pivotal couple", committed to having vowed in hope and love to take one man as a lifetime partner, and to dedicate that relationship before God. The theological question about marriage is not then for me an abstract one (few of the real ones are!) but a question of how I explain to myself or to anyone else the strangeness of such a commitment. For seventeen years of unsentimental living in all the emotional rough and tumble of family proximity, seeing friends' marriages break, and their sense that the awful pain was necessary as a way to regain any viable life, knowing devoted partners who find the idea of marriage repugnant and diminishing, recognising the constraints as well as the gifts of married life, forces me, at least, to acknowledge that such a commitment is strange.

To do theology about anything is, I believe, to set it in a framework which shows how it relates to that fusion of love and freedom which is God. If we demythologise theological ethics in this light, they become, not the commands of a directive supervisor, but the articulation of how certain modes of being and doing take us in the direction of that love/freedom, open us up to it, enable us to enact and image it, or challenge us to confession, to the recognition of our distance from fullness of life.

In the case of marriage, it seems to me, theology has a character-istically complex task, neither to defend marriage, nor to demonise it, but to explore how it relates to the aspects of the human condition which have a bearing on love and freedom. And there is no single or necessary account of that.

Marriage as natural relationship or cultural constraint: The doctrine of creation.

Traditional Roman Catholic and Reformation teaching about marriage is grounded in the man/wife relationship of Adam and Eve in the Genesis myth, and in the apparent endorsement of that relationship in the New Testament. Jesus is quoted in the Synoptic tradition as referring, apparently sympathetically, to the suggestion that a man or a woman leave father and mother to become one flesh. And his strictures on divorce seem to strengthen the permanence of the marital relationship rather than to weaken them, (though, significantly, they introduce a mutuality of entitlement to divorce not present in existing Jewish law.)

It is certainly clear that 'pair-bonding' occurs throughout nature, except in those creatures which can reproduce by parthenogenesis, or have a hermaphrodite biological structure. The range of variation on the monogamy to polygamy scale is wide, both within non-human and human species. Some birds, like gannets, are monogamous, and many human cultures are not.

There are many ways of reading this diversity theologically. One is to see the range, both animal and human, as part of the variety of God's creative patterning of life, and to accept it non-judgmentally. Another is to make a clear-cut distinction between all other species and the human, so that diversity in other animal life is seen as morally neutral, while human beings are susceptible to moral scrutiny, and monogamy is seen, distinctively for us, as normative. In both these cases, the theological understanding is that God sets natural parameters, in the other animals of irresistible instinct, but in humans of moral constraint which may or may not go against instinctual drives and desires. It is this sense of natural law which undergirds most traditional Catholic theology of marriage.

Against such readings of a given structure for human life, there is, in the theologies which wish to recognise post-modernist insights into the relativity of culture, an alternative possibility - that it belongs to the freedom which God gives to us in creation to make our cultures and their values. This is one possible reading of the responsibility given to Adam in the myth to be the namer of things, not the trivial sense of recognising a hippopotamus for what it was, and labelling it, but the profound responsibility of structuring the world by giving it linguistic, socio-political and cultural shape.

One major implication of that latter suggestion is that we do not find our ethics so much as make them, not by conscious or specific moments of choice, (certainly not in mono-cultural worlds which are pre-modern, and have not encountered the plurality of ethos, identity and structure which characterise our global village) but by the distinctive interpersonal creativity which gives the distinctive flavour and aroma to different times and places. Whether one is dismayed or excited by this suggestion is likely to be bound up with one's understanding of God, if one operates at all within a theological framework. If God is seen as jealous of human freedom, as one whose basic demand is for obedience to pre-ordained structures of nature and predetermined ethics, then the Fall consists of our refusal to accept these norms, our desire to set out on our own. This has certainly been the dominant Western reading of the Genesis myth, both Catholic and Protestant.

More endemic to Eastern Christian traditions is another reading of the myth, in which God is not jealous of our freedom, but anxious to maximise it, where the Fall is not so much the assertion of our freedom as the refusal to take the risks that involves, risks for example of not knowing but exploring, of receiving as gift the partiality of our finitude. The eating of the fruit of the forbidden tree is not sinister because God grudges us a share in his knowledge, or because it is sinful to desire to be as God. The sin is rather the will to short-circuit the responsibility for learning, by the exercise of our freedom, love and passion, the secrets of God: the desire to have them on a plate, refusing the stewardship of time and space, God's new gifts. Instant knowledge betrays our vocation.

Of course, it is quite possible, and probably the more common post-modernist stance, to assert the radical freedom human beings have to structure reality, but to see as quite redundant any idea of a transcendent source of this freedom. It is not my concern here to argue the apologetic corner for a realist account of God. Rather, from within a realist framework, I want to argue that there are understandings of God, deeply dependent on Scripture and tradition, which need not see God as the pre-determiner of things, including of right and wrong.

The question then arises, whether such understandings completely eliminate all sense of there being normative relationships, certainly ones which are defined in relation to a given nature. The structuralist suggestion is that 'nature' is itself a construct, and one which will not stand the scrutiny of comparative cultural and societal investigation. Certainly, Foucault argues, in the field of sexuality, that all specific relationships are constructed within a social milieu. And contemporary sociology of gender suggests that there is significant cultural control over our criteria of normal and natural behaviour or relationships. As with most analyses of causes, it is difficult to prove, without moving from evidence to dogma, that variable cultural factors are sufficient explanation of why life is patterned as it is. For me, cultural fatalism is as distasteful and unconvincing as any other sort. Yet the acknowledgement of human communities having widely different parameters to what they find natural seems clear as soon as one overhears the documentary comparisons.

One need not be a structuralist or a post-modernist, however, to argue that marriage is not a natural phenomenon. Both utopian anarchists and reluctant conformists have often suggested that marriage is an unnatural state, whether they accept or reject the social precepts to conform. It is a fairly conventional cynicism, perhaps more male than female, which Dr. Johnson expressed in a letter to Sir Joshua Reynolds:-

> It is so far from being natural for a man and a woman to live in a state of marriage that we find all the motives they have for remaining in that connection, and the restraints which civilised society imposes to prevent separation, are hardly sufficient to keep them together.

This line of argument has sometimes been used as a rationalisation of specifically male promiscuity, but it seems liable, when used about either sex, to suggest a negative ground for matrimony either in Blakean terms as the intrusive binding of natural desire or, with more Hobbesian approval, as the sort of constraint necessary to prevent chaos. More recent forms of the scepticism about marriage as a natural institution within contemporary European culture come from some social anthropologists, analysing the way shifts in education, mobility, longevity and self-understanding make serial relationships much likelier than strict lifelong monogamy.

No amount of description, however, settles the value question. Marriage may be relativised in our culture or others by other social modes of relating, but should it be? If one takes it that God's way of operation is not the issuing of cosmic fiats, but the invitation to discover liveable truth, is there any Christian middle-ground between absolutist ethics, and totally laissez-faire relativism?

I believe there is. The late 20th century has seen a remarkable recovery, in theoretical terms, (perhaps because we are so poor at the practice!) of the sense that we are relational beings. The biological and human sciences have been transformed by it, and philosophy and theology influenced by Buber, MacMurray and Zizioulas are beginning to challenge the atomism of post-Thatcherite Britain. In theological contexts, renewed attention to the doctrine of the Trinity, and to the associated theme of koinonia, communion, has suggested that the deepest anthropological truth about us is that we are, in the image of God, beings-who-relate.[1]

For much of Christian history, marriage has been defended largely for two reasons, one positive, the other negative; viz. the rearing of children and the containing of lust. Both, clearly, have biblical precedent as suggested grounds for the relationship's raison d'etre, though that very fact might be used as an illustration of how dangerous it is to identify isolated texts with the Word of God. That companionship and mutual cherishing should be a primary ground is a relatively modern notion, and interestingly, the most significant contemporary critique is that marriage has ceased, for various reasons, to be a likely context for such cherishing to be sustainable. The theologically vital core, it seems to me, undergirding the de facto variables of psychologically and culturally conditioned experiences of marriage, is that people are made for freedom and communion, and that all our human structures of relationship testify to that character of being. This is true even when specific relationships distort or caricature the intention of our human yearning.

Marriage as grace-bearing and sinful: Salvation

In Catholic tradition, marriage has become a sacrament. And in Reformed traditions, the wedding service speaks of 'holy matrimony'. Alongside Paul's somewhat grudging concession that marriage is better than burning, the New Testament, like the Jewish Scriptures, explores analogies between the husband/wife relationship and God's relationship to his bride, Israel, or Christ's to the new Israel, the Church. It is this holding of marriage as a microcosmic image of the selfgiving of God to his covenant people which gives it such high status in theological anthropology.

This iconography carries some conviction if it is read unsentimentally and unidealistically. The fidelity of God, and the responsive self-identification of his people as his has some echo, certainly, in the sense of mutuality and belonging which love generates. Yet it is a mutuality which includes the deepest negativities of betrayal, anger and disappointment, and commits both God and people to passion, not in the Mills and Boon sense of the word, but in the prophetic and Christological sense. For such bonding, involving the commitment to stand with the other identified in solidarity through thick and thin, has to be seen as some kind of self-transcendence. It is not, however, self-abnegation, for at a deeper level than the pain is recognition that somehow, in freedom, identities have become interdependent, so that they do not have their life as units, but only in mutuality.

In a culture so fiercely aware of individual rights and freedoms, such talk may sound extremely sinister. We prefer an anthropology of self-making, self-sufficiency and self-management, a secure base of intact identity from which we then choose to move out into relationships. We are well aware of the romantic myths of coupledom, of "two halves", of the pastoral, therapeutic task of restoring self-esteem to those who have been swallowed by bad marriages which have obliterated them; of destructive dependence; of rationalised inequity.

Nevertheless, if we are, as Christians, to offer an account of marriage deeper than that of mutual, and possibly lifelong convenience, it must be in terms of learning, tasting, and treasuring a relationship which is constituted by the will and desire to risk such committed belonging that we let it change our identity. We are no longer ourselves by ourselves. It is this vulnerability and the finding of joy in it, which makes marriage potentially grace-bearing.

In Western romanticism, the ideologising of the experience of falling in love means that most marriages are contracted in that happy and euphoric period of relationship when commitment seems effortless and as natural as breathing, when sexual adrenaline is at its peak, and when the distinguishing of loving from being in love seems inconceivable. Yet, as cultures where arranged marriages are the norm well testify, the 'success' of a marriage may follow as well from learning to love as from finding that one already does. And as marriage counsellors even in our soap opera culture often recognise, strong marriages survive what is often a phase of 'being in love' and, need not be ashamed of the fact that that stage is recognisably passed. The question, 'Are you no longer in love with your wife/husband?' is doubtless as alarming to many as the question, "Have you stopped beating your wife yet?" In particularly gifted marriages, that sense may survive a lifetime. In all but the saddest, it will be rediscovered often enough to sustain the sense of preciousness, the remarkableness of this other person whom habit and wear and tear so easily dull into ordinariness. But in between, the psychological ranges of what keep a marriage a living gift and not a gruesome bondage may vary immensely. Communication, comradeship, shared activities, polar opposition of temperament, sexual chemistry, loving commitment to children may all be more or less present.

What is grace-full about marriage is not the degree of giftedness there is about any of these specifics or their sum. Of course, our natural happiness is bound up with them very closely: and the well-being of two people who mellow in the exchange of life and find themselves fruitful in those various dimensions is one of the enviable human scenarios. But what manifests grace in a marriage is that it is, in Christian terms, a microcosm of the mutual solidarity between God and creation, which generates commitment through thick and thin, and for which we depend on resourcing from a love deeper than even our own natural instincts. Whether or not it is named as God, or Christ, who provides the resource is secondary. The point is that, without underestimating the resilience and devotion of the human spirit, Christians locate such renewal of love in the infinity of God's own.

It has been part of the rubric of Christian marriage, character-istically, that it defends this solidarity by insisting on exclusiveness 'forsaking all other'. This, of course is primarily sexual, but it carries normally the further implication that it is this relationship

which takes priority in a person's life over all others, which
properly claims the prime time, the deepest communication etc.
For many, an ongoingly happy marriage is one where this is true,
no matter how much else two people do separately or outside
the marriage. For many, perceived infidelities of time or
communication erode, even more insistently than sexual infidelity,
the sense of breakdown in relationship. Long past the stage of
enchanted conviction that this woman/man is, as they say 'the whole
world to me' marriage is a prioritised relationship Whereas a spouse
may be able to accept that in some aspects, this or that other
relationship nourishes the partner more than the marriage does,
(say in intellectual stimulus, or in musical companionship, or in
political commitment), it would spell disaster for most marriages if
the subliminal message came through that all in all, someone else
was more important to the other. And, specifically, the recognition
that someone else was more important to the other sexually, whether
in experience or in desire, would threaten to shatter most marriages.

It is precisely this necessarily safeguarded intimacy which,
ironically, seems to me to make marriage also sinful, not in the
trivial sense of immoral and to be avoided, but in the profound
cosmic sense of sinful, that it manifests our inextricable
embeddedness in a limitation of love which cannot be projected as
our hoped-for end state. For this reason, though I am, most of the
time, glad to be married; and though I have no moral guilt about
having chosen it, I hope that Jesus was right, or the redactor who
gave him the line, that in the Kingdom of God, we neither marry,
nor are given in marriage. For it seems to me that, however we
envisage the state of redeemed co-existence, in or out of time, it
cannot be properly envisaged as a place of excluding relationships,
even if it is hoped for as a condition of transformed particularity,
in which identity is sustained, recognisably continuous with our
present identity.

For many, speculation about afterlife belongs to the realm of
religious fantasy, a clear case of myth. I am agnostic about what a
Jewish student once called 'the protocol of heaven'; but it does
seem to me that if we want, as I do, to maintain a realist, though
not empiricist account of the presence of the living Christ, we are
entitled to hope for a comparable realism about our own presence
to one another in God. But I am quite sure that, if such life is
possible, the character of the transformation involved in our access
to it will involve our becoming capable of bearing the generosity of

God. And that, I am sure will mean that even our best particularity of relationship becomes transparent to the presence of others, intentionally and willingly inclusive.

If, on the other hand, talk of life after death is read as myth, the importance of the saying about not marrying in the kingdom of heaven is to plot the existential distance between our exclusive relationships and the thrust towards inclusiveness which characterises kingdom-talk at its best, and kingdom-living at its most compelling.

Eschatology and ethics: Practice and procedure.

This account is, so far, intended to be provocative and personal rather than comprehensive and descriptive. The documentation of Reformed theology on the subject is dense and accessible in the archive reports of many churches, and there is widespread recognition of the general church position being, at least of officially, 'No sex except in the context of heterosexual marriage'. So what follows ethically from this placing of marriage as a socially constructed way of relating, which manifests in its intention the constancy of shared life which images God's constancy, and yet, by its exclusiveness cannot quite represent God's generosity?

It seems to me that there is no direct deductive route from eschatology to ethics. Even if one's vision of the kingdom is clearly suggestive of a transformation of present structures, it does not follow that that transformation can be morally engineered. We walk a knife-edge between moral complacency, which shrugs off the domestication of sin, and rejects the leverage of the kingdom, and on the other side, utopian striving, which short-circuits the conditions of earthly existence, and generally blows all the moral fuses around. The delicacy of exploring what Paul meant by sinning boldly is the key skill here.

The reason why Jesus worried and worries the legalists is that he cared far more about the inwardness of action than about its accessible public rating. He seemed to have risked a kind of flexibility, particularly in relation to the socially stigmatised, which upset moral absolutists. This was in no way moral indifferentism, but a kind of rejection of external judgement which thought it had good and evil taped (again attempting to bypass the long pilgrimage of understanding the complex freedom of being human, by swallowing instant apples of the knowledge of good and evil).

If we are to operate in the mode of Christ in relation to people's human and domestic relationships, we have to wrestle with the following recognitions:-

> There are many people in technically impeccable marriages who would nevertheless experience them as bleak and formal relationships.

> There are many people for whom brief affairs, or even one-night stands give a glimpse of the overcoming of loneliness, or the possibility of joy, albeit unsustainable.

> There are many people for whom marriage is impossible, either epidemiologically, or for psychological, social or cultural reasons.

If marriage is to be commended, it must be because of its visible strength as a relationship of enabling mutuality. It cannot be commended as an arbitrary divine fiat, or out of fear. Alongside its commendation must go recognition of how often marriage has supported, and even helped to generate patriarchal attitudes; and of the dangers of possessiveness and 'couple introversion' which leave others, particularly the single, feeling second-class citizens.

While it is part of the Christian vision of sexuality that it belongs best in a context of secure loving, rather than one of exploitation, or trivial self-gratification, we must attend to the motives and hopes of those who reject marriage for idealistic reasons, or out of disillusionment with the way they see marriage function all around them. The idealism may be naive, overestimating the strength of other relationships, but it must not be scorned, especially not by those who acknowledge the track record of marriage as a highly ambiguous institution.

Given candour about all these factors, theology can still make positive and distinctive affirmations about marriage. In the pastoral mode, it can, of course, share with other secular disciplines insights into strategies for better rather than worse marriages. It can de-mystify marriage, and remove it from any kind of pedestal which suggests that married people have exclusive or priority access to grace, love or participation in the koinonia of God. But more significantly, it can deepen the understanding of marriage from being a common human structuring of natural affection, and a widespread channelling of sexual desire, so that the commitment is seen as pointing towards the inexhaustibility of the divine love.

But people, and relationships are exhaustible. Vows, no matter how solemnly taken, do not guarantee the creativity which makes a living marriage. And once the relationship is sustained only by the sense of obedience to the vows, (though that may be a short-term help for dealing with sticky patches), it has actually, existentially, died. Tragic as this usually is for those who have entered the relationship with hope and good intent, it cannot be redeemed by metaphysical strictures about the two being inseparable in Christ.

Learning that we live on earth and not in heaven, accepting the fragility of even our best relationships, knowing that we cannot sustain the weight of the lightness of God's freedom, all this involves us in a proper provisionality about ethical norms. It invites us to self-forgiveness, and certainly to refusal to scold the fragile world. It is a matter of vocation, of delicate and subtle discernment, to discover how each of us bears witness to both the eschatological vision and to the challenge of earthed life. Some will marry, hopefully testifying to the fidelity of love, but recognising ruefully that this exclusive loving is in some ways an ironic image of a prodigally loving God. Some will refuse marriage as an act of narrowing, but recognising ruefully that transitory relationships are an ironic image of a constant God. And most will discover, though this may be in part a function of social expectations and responses, that flesh and blood find it hard to handle eternal triangles, let alone eschatological polygons. But even there, there may be some who risk exploring other patterns of personal and sexual co-existence, not from carelessness or self-indulgence, but because they find themselves called there in the integrity of their own love and freedom. There is, I suspect, all the difference in the world between a deceitful affair, betraying the trust of one partner, and the emotional and even sexual openness of those rare people who have worked through to a sense of unpossessiveness which allows them to transcend normal human jealousies.

Many presuppositions float underneath the surface icebergs of this essay. All of them demand further scrutiny. I have not justified, but simply assumed a hermeneutical stance which makes Scripture liable to questions about cultural limitations. I have not proved, but simply affirmed that the perspective of those who challenge marriage as an irretrievably flawed structure deserve attention, not demonisation. And I have not proved but simply affirmed that those of us who still live married are able to do so in good faith, provided we purge ourselves of complacency and triumphalism. What I hope this essay may do is to tease those who pick up the book into the sort of confusion which my old Moral Philosophy professor called "the initial sign of progress in philosophy"!

---

1 For example, J Zizioulas, *Being as Communion*

For the procreation of children

David Hilborn

In early 1993, my wife gave birth to our first child, a son. He was delivered in a modern hospital with considerable help from medical science. He arrived in the fifth year of our marriage and was very much a 'planned' baby. We had always hoped to have children and believed they would enhance our relationship. We had discussed what we might do if either of us proved infertile and had agreed that if certain 'artificial' methods failed, we would apply for adoption. Since both of us felt called to continue working after the birth, we made appropriate childcare arrangements for part of each day. Becoming Christian parents has changed more than just our daily routine: it has made us reassess our domestic, social and spiritual priorities.

Of course, these reflections are anecdotal and every couple's experience of parenthood is different. Nonetheless, they beg important questions about the theology of marriage in regard to children. To what extent is reproduction a 'purpose' of marriage? Are couples obliged to bear offspring? Where do sex and contraception fit into the picture? How is matrimony linked to 'family life'? How far should we go in allowing technology to facilitate childbirth? How much are gender roles defined by childrearing? And what does procreation tell us about the purpose and nature of God?

The place of procreation in marriage

'Children', said the Psalmist, 'are a reward from the Lord' (*Psalm 127:3*). This may be hard to believe when changing a nappy at 4am, but the Old Testament frequently depicts procreation as both a blessing and a sacred duty of husband and wife. As such, it occupies a central place in many of the covenants made between God and his people, where faithfulness is closely linked to strong lineage (*eg. Genesis 9:1-11; Genesis 15:1-21*). In ancient Israel, it was taken for granted that all who married would observe the key creation ordinance of *Genesis 1:28* to 'be fruitful and multiply'. The imperative to reproduce was so powerful that it overrode allegiance to a particular marital bond and thus became a prime justification for polygamy, concubinage and divorce

(*Genesis 16:1-4; Genesis 30:1-5; Exodus 21:7-11; Deuteronomy 24:1ff*). [1]

As a whole, the New Testament perpetuates the assumption that marriage will produce offspring (*Matthew 7:9-11; Luke 12:52-53; I Timothy 3:4,12*). Nevertheless, the teachings of Jesus on wedlock focus not on its procreational significance, but rather on those relational aspects stressed in the second creation story (*Matthew 19:1-12; Mark 10:6-9; cf. Genesis 2:4ff*). This emphasis on matrimony as a 'one flesh' union is exemplified by his disavowal of infertility as a cause for divorce (*Matthew 19:9, cf. Malachi 2:14-16*).

The priority of procreation is further qualified in the New Testament by expectations about 'the end of the age'. Jesus declares in *Luke 20:34-35* that the closeness of the Kingdom makes marriage a finite option rather than an absolute obligation, and in the next verse true 'childhood' is cast not literally, but metaphorically in relation to faith in God and the resurrection of the dead. A similar urgency underlies Paul's advice to the Corinthians that unmarried men should 'not seek a wife' because marriage and family responsibilities might distract them from the 'Lord's affairs' (*1 Corinthians 7:29-35*).

The biblical tension between fruitfulness and devotion to the kingdom is very much mirrored in the history of church teaching on marriage and procreation. Influenced by neo-Platonic ideals of 'renouncing the world', many early Christian Fathers inferred from Jesus and Paul that while marriage may be necessary and permissible for most, celibacy was a purer form of discipleship. While such notions were not meant to impugn marriage as such, they served to lend it a somewhat pragmatic and expedient image. It was justified not on its own terms, but only insofar as it served some 'higher purpose' - and more often than not this higher purpose was the procreation of children. Most influentially, it was the work of Augustine on marriage which confirmed its first aim as reproduction while at the same time making its 'conjugal' and 'sacramental' dimensions secondary to this end.[2] What is more, the key impact of Augustine's teaching on the Reformation ensured that this order of priorities was preserved in certain early Protestant rites, the marriage service in the *Book of Common Prayer* being a good example:

> First [marriage] was ordained for the procreation of children,
> to be brought up in the fear and nurture of the Lord, and to the
> praise of his Holy name. Secondly, it was ordained for a
> remedy against sin, and to avoid fornication ... Thirdly, it was
> ordained for the mutual society, help and comfort, that one
> ought to have of one another.

Broadly speaking, since the Reformation, Catholicism has
maintained a 'primary' position for procreation in the purposes of
married life, while Protestantism has moved away from the view
that it comes before any other marital imperative.[3] Reformed
churches have especially tended to highlight matrimony as a model
of companionship and social cohesion rather than as the proper
vehicle for progeniture. John Calvin was certainly alive to these
interpersonal facets of marriage and it is worth pointing out that
whereas Martin Luther saw women chiefly as child bearers and
divinely-appointed means of venereal relief, Calvin was readier to
present them as inseparable and lifelong 'partners' with men.[4]
Today it is possible to discern a consensus among Protestant
churches that marriage is far more to do with the two people who
covenant together as husband and wife than with any children they
might happen to produce. In view of the 'qualitative' New
Testament emphasis mentioned above, and with Western divorce
rates creeping over 40%,[5] this is surely a healthy approach. 2000
years on, Christian couples might not so readily cite the return of
Christ as a reason for subordinating procreation to their own piety.
Nonetheless, there is a real sense in which the coming kingdom
redefines all human relationships in terms of 'value' rather than
'productivity', and so mitigates the overwhelming compulsion to
beget descendants which we find running through the Law of
Moses. As Karl Barth once put it, the 'pressure' to bear offspring
has been removed by the fact that the 'Son on whose birth
everything seriously and ultimately depended has now been born
and become our Brother'.[6]

Procreation, sex and contraception

While Christ's emphasis on marriage as a 'one flesh' partnership
may allow us to place its relational quality before its procreative
capacity, it is nonetheless true that these two dimensions are linked.
If sexual intercourse is held to be the supreme expression of
matrimonial commitment, we must acknowledge at one and the
same time that it is intrinsically procreative. This does not mean,

of course, that every sexual act leads to conception, but it does recognise that in all natural cases, it is through sex that children are conceived. Not surprisingly, perhaps, this combination of purposes is highly charged and emotive. Neither would it be an exaggeration to say that it has led to profound theological confusion. From the earliest Fathers onwards, doctrines of marriage have struggled to reconcile the divinely-sanctioned business of reproduction with that range of intense passions and urges which is displayed in intercourse. Again, it was Augustine who was quintessential here, failing as he did to differentiate between sex as a God-given blessing for married life and sex as a repository of fallen, sinful desire. Indeed, while he saw intercourse as justified when practised explicitly for procreation, even this was thought to bear an ineradicable taint of 'concupiscence', or depraved lust, deriving from the original sin of Adam and Eve.[7]

Today, of course, such extreme ascetic perspectives are largely discredited. The widespread use of contraception - whether natural or artificial - has deeply affected modern theologies of marriage and has stimulated both Catholics and Protestants to regard sex as crucial in its own right, for the mutual enrichment of husband and wife. Within Christian partnerships, it is now hardly controversial to suggest that genuine sensual pleasure can be redeemed from the hold that sin undoubtedly still has on many areas of sexual life and that as such, it does not need the supposedly 'greater good' of childbirth to validate it. If anything in fact, when the New Testament gives 'reasons' for wedlock, it does so by referring to natural impulses quite apart from any association with childbearing. We have already noted that Jesus treats marriage relationally rather than procreatively, but it is the blunt advice of Paul to 'marry rather than burn with passion' which strikes home most directly (*1 Corinthians 7:9*).

From what we have seen so far, it would appear neither that sex need be morally justified by procreation, nor that marriage need be morally justified by childbirth. Having said this, it is still important to discern how the physical dependence of conception on intercourse relates to God's providence. In other words, while a Christian couple might be helped by distinguishing their sexual relationship from their biological potential to reproduce, is there not all the same a paradigmatic, or even a sacramental, connection between the two? As the American Methodist Paul Ramsey once inquired, 'in the mystery of our beings, God has joined our sexuality and our procreativity) together. Ought (we) ever to put them asunder?' [8]

Procreation, children and family life

It is a plain fact that the great majority of marriages at some time or other produce children. In England and Wales alone, more than 80% of all adult females have borne children and when one considers that in 1990 three-quarters of UK births took place within wedlock, it is clear that marriage and procreation are closely allied. Indeed the 'nuclear' unit of 'husband, wife and kid/s' is still by far the most common British household type.[9] Statistics are not available to show whether the proportion of Christian couples with children is higher than average, but given the copious scriptural and ecclesiastical approval of fertility, one might suppose that it is. Clearly, none of this is in itself sufficient to confirm that God requires all couples who are capable of reproducing to do so. Nonetheless, it does largely bear out what scripture assumes and anthropology implies - namely that procreation is a characteristic corollary of marriage.

Now quite obviously, once having identified this pattern, we must be mindful of the exceptions - quite apart from those circumstances in which partners are simply incapable of reproducing due to age, sterility and so on. From a Christian point of view, there are certain very good reasons why a fertile husband and wife may decide against 'trying for a baby'. For example, the woman's health may be at severe risk from pregnancy and/or childbirth. Similarly, a child who is conceived may be seriously threatened by congenital disease. In some cases, the special vocation of one or both partners may render procreation reckless and unfair on any children who might result. Beyond such clear exceptions, however, there are several circumstances in which the reasoning might be more theologically suspect. In an increasingly materialistic age, many couples forego children for economic reasons, either because they do not feel able to provide for a son or daughter, or because starting a family would adversely affect their own career or standard of living. St Paul may have valued 'well-managed households' (*1 Timothy 3:4-5; 12*), but any decision against children which is determined by money, status and possessions risks flying in the face of Christ's core teaching in the Sermon on the Mount: 'Do not store up treasures on earth';

'You cannot serve both God and money', and 'Do not worry about what you will eat, drink and wear' (*Matthew 6:19, 24, 25*). For the Christian, parenthood is an act of faith and trust before it is a calculation, and it would be wrong to suppose that a 'responsible' approach to it has more to do with finance and position than prayer and self-sacrifice. My wife delivered our son at a time when our joint income had considerably decreased, and I doubt whether we would have learned as much about God's provision if this had not been so.

Equally open to question is that refusal to have children which derives from a professed 'dislike' or 'aversion' to them. While often quite genuine, this outlook can also represent a form of selfishness and misanthropy which is incompatible with gospel principles. Quite possibly too, it might stem from a spouse's own unhappy childhood, in which case it is important to be aware that hurts are being rationalised which in fact need to be healed.

A more studied case for childlessness is sometimes made by those who claim that for various reasons, this world is too awful a place for children. Whether because of overpopulation, pollution, the bomb or whatever, it is reckoned that they should not be left so chronic a legacy as the planet earth in its current state. While such arguments may accompany acute moral awareness, one must wonder how seriously they take the sovereignty of God in the unfolding of history. After all, Jesus himself was born at a time of turmoil, conflict and oppression, and though he described the Apocalypse as unfavourable for 'pregnant women and nursing mothers' (*Matthew 24:19*), he was dismissive of those who based their lives on too absolute and rigid an apocalyptic code (*Mark 13:32-37*). On a positive level, one might argue that raising children can cultivate in us a more conscious and active regard for peace, ecology and justice, since these are then likely to become rather more than matters of enlightened self-interest. Even in the face of population growth, parents who 'plan' a modest family could be said more realistically to represent a proper global strategy than those who rule out children altogether.

Undoubtedly, it is a couple's motives and intentions which are vital in any assessment of their remaining childless by choice. Just as contraception can enhance our God-given capacity to 'steward' or regulate childbirth, so deciding against children can in certain instances represent a godly exercise of freewill. Indeed, if childless partners' intentions are righteous, there is no reason to suppose that they will 'put asunder' the essential relationship between marriage and procreation since, as we have already shown, this relationship is universal and woven into the order of creation, rather than being particularly dependent on the fruitfulness of any one union.

By way of reflection on these arguments, it is worth noting that too literally 'child-centred' a definition of marriage is in any case challenged by Jesus' own radical redescriptions of 'the family' in such texts as *Matthew 19:29, Luke 14:26 and Mark 3:33-34*. Here, it appears that Christ makes generational ties secondary to those ties of faith which distinguish the new 'household' of God from all earthly patterns of domestic life. Not only do such texts stand in judgement over contemporary rhetoric about 'family values': they further underline that matrimony is to be reckoned according to the quality of its spiritual and ethical demeanour, rather than according to the quantity of its issue.

Procreation, infertility and 'artificial' reproduction

Having examined the pros and cons of voluntary childlessness, it is sadly ironic to recall that many married people are desperate to have children, but are physically unable to do so. 'Infertility' might now be defined as a failure to conceive after one year of regular intercourse without the use of contraceptives, but the pain and stigma it arouses have direct antecedents in the 'barrenness' we find portrayed so negatively in the Old and New Testaments. Whether endured by Sarah (*Genesis 17:15ff*), Rachel (*Genesis 30:1-8*), Hannah (*1 Samuel 1:5ff*) or Elizabeth (*Luke 1:7ff*), the Bible casts this as a wretched affliction curable only by the miraculous intervention of God. Today, the anguish of those who cannot have children seems undiminished: during the course of my wife's pregnancy, no less than four couples we knew were coming to terms with infertility, and all of them required the most sensitive pastoral care. By contrast, the effect of 'miracles' on this problem now seems more widely discerned in the way modern science has addressed it, that in any apologetic for divine intervention. The last 20 years in particular have been marked by what Peter Singer and Deane Wells[10] call a 'Reproductive Revolution' - one in which a bewildering array of artificial techniques have raised several new ethical problems.

In Christian terms, the general principle of 'assisted' conception can be welcomed. Once we accept that not every act of intercourse exists for procreation, it is at least possible to maintain that not every act of procreation need derive from intercourse. Furthermore, if children are as much a part of God's purpose for marriage as we have observed them to be, we can surely detect his hand in those medical advances designed to enhance fertility and/or enable fertilisation of a wife's eggs by her husband's sperm. Both Artificial Insemination by the Husband (AIH) and In Vitro Fertilisation (IVF) using the ova and semen of a married couple would fall into this category.

Severe theological difficulties emerge, however, once a 'third party' enters the reproductive process - either 'anonymously', as in Artificial Insemination by Donor (AID) and IVF using donated sperm, donated eggs or both, or more immediately, as in the various forms of surrogate parenthood. What all these procedures have in common is that they remove procreation from the relational 'two in one' context of wedlock. Rather than 'forsaking all others', they co-opt an outsider into one or both of two formative marital acts - procreation and intercourse. Even if we accept that these techniques fall short of 'adultery' because they lack the elements of lust and betrayal; even if we argue that Hagar, for instance, was used by Abraham and Sarah as a 'surrogate mother', it is hard to reconcile 'third party' fertilisation with the teaching of Jesus - most particularly if the third party in question gains financially from being involved. Granted, the quality of a child's nurture is of greater moral concern that its genetic make-up: after all, Christ loved, blessed and exalted children without regard to their 'legitimacy' (*Mark 10:14; Matthew 18:3*). Neither, as we have seen, is our blood-line of decisive significance in the community of those 'born again' by water and the Spirit (*John 3:5-6*). But on this basis, it is surely preferable for a sterile that is, permanently infertile) couple to seek adoption, thereby preserving their exclusive physical contract with one another while giving themselves in love and care to one who might otherwise be less fortunate.

God, man and woman in procreation

Insofar as procreation is a fundamental command of God, it is issued against a background of his having made us 'in his image' (*Genesis 1:27-28*). Most obviously, this implies an analogy of

29

action: God creates and orders the universe, and places upon men and women a special responsibility to 'fill the earth and subdue it' (*Genesis 1:28*). There is also, however, an analogy of being at work here - or rather, an analogy of being-in-relation. The image of God is not monolithic, but interpersonal: 'male and female created he them'. Similarly, in the Yahwist account, Eve is introduced as a 'helper' for Adam - someone with whom he can share his humanity, his love, his labour and his discourse (*Genesis 2:18*). It is interesting that the major divisions of gender which emerge in this second story do so only after Adam and Eve have rebelled against God: childbearing appears to have been an attribute of woman from the start, but the pain which goes with it, like her subjection to her husband, stems directly from temptation and sin (*Genesis 2:16; 3:8ff*).

The implications of all this would seem to be that while basic God-given physiology predetermines male-female roles in reproduction, there is no such divine 'blueprint' for the domestic and social functions which have been assigned to men and women as a result. No doubt, primitive societies were ordered largely along sexual lines: women were home-makers because they bore and fed the next generation, while men, possessing greater build and visual-spatial skill, took responsibility for hunting food and defending the tribe. The key issue for a modern theology of marriage is whether these anatomically-based distinctions need any longer determine the patterns of society and family life. Contemporary Western culture is now far removed from the tribal, hunter-gathering model, and offers many less gender-specific means of 'breadwinning'. In addition, with the refinement of contraception, and especially with the advent of the pill during the 1960's, sexually active women have for the first time in their history been able to opt out of a probable twenty or thirty-year cycle of birth and nurture, and have in unprecedented numbers combined marriage and motherhood with a career.

Such developments compel us to distinguish between the biological prerequisites of procreation and their subsequent institutionalis-ation. Indeed, given the original extent of Eve's mutuality with Adam, and bearing in mind the Reformed insistence that sin has deeply defiled God's image in us,[11] it might well be argued that the proper 'redeemed' Christian approach to childcare is a genuinely shared division of tasks. Ideally, this would mean that each spouse was employed part-time instead of the husband being always 'at work' and a wife always 'at home'. Clearly, harsh economic realities will often make this impossible - although it is worth reiterating that 'financial comfort' fails to convince as a pre-requisite for the Christian planning a family. Furthermore, while each partner must obviously accentuate their own particular skills and adopt those roles which best serve their relationship, they should beware of conforming too easily to the 'pattern of this world' (*Romans 12:2*), with its tendency towards sexual stereotyping and the sort of fixed model of 'family life' which Jesus challenged so forcefully.

Inasmuch as marriage is a model of human creativity and human community, it reflects to some extent the creativity and community of God himself. As Trinity, he resembles husband and wife by being both united in substance and diverse in personhood; as Maker and Sustainer of heaven and earth, he both engenders life and nurtures it; in male terms, he is Father, Abba, Son, Lord, and Master; in female terms, Wisdom, Israel's 'mother' (*Isaiah 66:13*) and Jerusalem's hen-like protector (*Matthew 23:37*).

Ultimately, of course, God is beyond gender and analogy, and we should avoid drawing too many parallels between his existence and the character of marriage, reproduction and family life. For God, creation is not a necessity whereas for us it is an indispensable feature of our existence. Jesus' conception by the Holy Spirit and birth of a virgin distinguish him from the rest of humanity rather than identifying him with it, while being 'eternally begotten of the Father' marks his life off starkly from our own.

The 'otherness' of God is also crucially apparent in that while children may be conceived by human parents, God alone brings about a greater conception - one in which we are born 'not of blood nor of the will of man' (*John 1:12-13*) and in which we are thus without physical descent (*Hebrews 7:3*). This greater conception is conception to eternal life, and it can only be achieved by 'leaving parents behind' (*Matthew 10: 37-78; 12:46-49*). In this sense, we can conclude that just as offspring must eventually 'depart from father and mother' (*Genesis 2:24*), so father and mother must 'let go' of their children in order that they, too, might be 'fruitful' - not only in marriage and procreation, but also in saving faith and Christian discipleship.

1   Rabbis disagreed about this text's application - a disagreement which is echoed in the Pharisees' question to Jesus at Matthew 19:3. While the school of Shammai held a wife's adultery to be the only valid reason for divorce, followers of Hillel allowed husbands to choose from a far wider range of causes see A.H. Mc'Neile, *The Gospel according to Matthew*, St Martin's Press, 1965, p.272).

2   Augustine, *De Nuptia et Concupiscentia 1*.

3   For an expansion and qualification of this distinction see P. Ramsey, *One Flesh,* Grove Booklet on Ethics No. 8, Bramcote, 1975, p.7ff.

4   Compare eg. Calvin's *Commentary on Genesis* 2:18 with Luther's 'Letter to three nuns' in his *Letters of Spiritual Counsel,* ed. T.G. Tappert, 1955, p.271.

5   Source: *Social Trends 22* (1992) Ed. T Griffin, HMSO.

6   *Church Dogmatics III/4, The doctrine of reconciliation* Ed. G.W. Bromiley and T.F. Torrance, T & T Clark, 1961, p.266.

7   *De civitate Dei* 14.26.

8   P. Ramsey, op. cit. p.7.

9   Source: *Social Trends 22* (1992) op. cit. p.42.

10 P. Singer and D. Wells, *The Reproductive Revolution* OUP, 1984.

11 J. Calvin, *Institutes* I: xv:1-4. Ed. J.T. McNeill, Westminster Press, 1960.

Pulling down the idol:
Lesbian and gay relationships and marriage
Elizabeth Stuart

During the last thirty years all the major Christian denominations
in Britain have had to grapple with the issue of homosexuality.
Medical, psychological and sociological studies have challenged
traditional and scriptural understandings of homosexuality as a
deliberate perversion or a mental or physical disease. It seems that
the phenomenon of people orientated emotionally and sexually
primarily towards members of their own sex is consistently present
as a small percentage of every population. Such men and women
seem to suffer no more mental or physical ill-health than
heterosexual people and most live decent and 'ordinary' lives.
As well as having to come to terms with this scientific data the
Churches have also been afforded an unprecedented insight into
the lives of gay men and lesbian women by those gay and lesbian
people, among them Christians of all hues, who have taken the
brave step of 'coming out', publicly acknowledging themselves
as lesbian or gay (despite living in a society riddled with fear,
ignorance and hatred of homosexuality). In the face of the reality
of lesbian and gay lives and relationships common assumptions
explode - such as the assumption that all lesbians and especially
gay men are inherently promiscuous and cannot sustain a stable,
monogamous relationship, or that such people are only attracted
to partners considerably younger than themselves, or that gay or
lesbian couples assume 'masculine' and 'feminine' roles.

All this has led many Christian Churches to reassess their attitudes
to homosexuality. Working parties within at least some of them
have gone as far as to suggest that lesbian and gay relationships are
not necessarily sinful and can generate great love, joy and stability
to the people involved and to those around them. In 1991 a
working party convened by the central committee of the Church
and Society Department of the United Reformed Church produced
a report which did not receive any official endorsement but which
concluded nevertheless that,

> Our instinct is to affirm grace against law as a general rule,
> to take the risks of acceptance rather than those of rejection,
> to seek for humility rather than a righteousness tending
> towards self-righteousness.[1]

However no mainstream denomination in this country has yet felt able to offer lesbian and gay people an official Church blessing of their relationship and all Christian denominations continue to promote marriage as the ideal Christian relationship. Gay and lesbian couples, whatever the quality of their love, 'fall short' of this ideal. God's primary aim for men and women is that they come together in loving, monogamous, permanent relationships which may result in the bringing to birth of children. It is in and through this relationship that the nature of the love of God most clearly manifests itself. Gay and lesbian people are presumably meant to feel sad that they cannot realize this ideal - or perhaps to stop 'practising' as homosexuals and conform superficially to the heterosexual model.

I believe that gay and lesbian people have enormous gifts to bring to Christian communities and one of those gifts is prophetic insight. People pushed to the margins of institutions (for whatever reason) are often able to see what is actually going on in them with a clarity unavailable to those in the middle. Those of us who are gay or lesbian find this talk about marriage as the ideal difficult to swallow. One in three marriages in Britain end in divorce, the average length of this supposedly life-long commitment is just over nine years. During the last ten years we have learnt what a dangerous place marriage can be. Women have murdered their husbands to escape a hell of mental and physical abuse and children have been driven to court to seek a separation from their parents. For those of us on the outside looking in, the 'ideal' seems far from ideal for millions of men and women and children; instead of bringing them 'shalom' - happiness, peace, wholeness and love - it brings them pain, disillusionment, brokenness. The tragic spectacle of the royal family being torn apart as the fairy tale marriages turn sour, splinter and become living nightmares symbolizes what is going on in millions of homes throughout the land. And yet the Churches continue to promote the 'ideal', blaming the breakdown of marriages on human frailty and sin, and millions of men and women continue to search for the ideal through second and even third or fourth marriages.

If any other institution was going so wrong and causing so much unhappiness one would hope that the Churches would ask serious questions about its nature and validity but marriage seems to be beyond criticism in Christian circles. In a sense it has become an idol rather than an ideal. All are expected to acknowledge its goodness and greatness, no matter what their experience. All are expected to sacrifice themselves to it in one way or another and when things go wrong everyone but the idol is to blame. Anyone questioning its status is regarded as dangerous and subversive. Like Moses returning to his people at the bottom of Mount Sinai gay and lesbian people stand at the sidelines and watch as thousands of men, women and children are sacrificed to the golden calf of marriage. Why should we too sacrifice ourselves to this ideal by abstaining from the sexual relationships that have meaning for us or by acknowledging that our relationships could never live up to this ideal.

The American psychologist M. Scott Peck has written that 'Mental health is an ongoing process of dedication to reality at all costs.'[2] In the biblical tradition prophets are people chosen by God to recall his people to reality and therefore to mental health. I believe that lesbian and gay people in our day are called to assume the prophetic mantle and recall all society, but particularly the Church, to the reality of human relationships. As people living outside the institution of marriage,[3] like the boy in the tale they can see that the emperor has no clothes, that marriage is not an ideal relationship for many. And in their own persons they ask an uncomfortable question of the Church - would the God of love revealed in the person of Jesus of Nazareth exclude millions of men and women from the possibility of experiencing the fullness of love by focussing that experience only within marriage?

So far I have painted an entirely gloomy picture of marriage. But we all know that there are many marriages that do work, where hard work and commitment does bear fruit in a relationship suffused with mutuality and reciprocity which mirrors and incarnates the love of God for creation. This is truly the ideal realized. We need to ask, if marriage itself does not automatically realize this ideal, what relationship is it, at the base of happy marriages, that does realize the ideal?

In my experience if you ask a happily married couple the secret of the success of their relationship and you will almost certainly get the reply, 'we are friends' or 'he/she is my best friend'. It is in the friendship between the man and woman that both are transformed into 'one flesh' and transfigured into sacraments of God's love. Where there is no friendship or friendship breaks down the sacrament is lost and so is the transforming power of the relationship. I would argue that it is not marriage itself that is the ideal Christian relationship but friendship. This is a reality that lesbian and gay people can teach the Churches. Few Christians who take the trouble to get to know lesbian and gay people could deny that they are capable of forming relationships which put many marriages to shame, relationships that are obviously good for those involved and those around them, relationships based upon mutuality and reciprocity in which God is very obviously present. These are not marriages but they display the characteristics of good marriages. Ask a happy gay and lesbian couple the secret of their success and they will probably give you exactly the same answer as their heterosexual counterparts: 'friendship'. Happy gay and lesbian couples by their very existence challenge Churches to face the fact that they have idealized the wrong relationship, idolized an institution and obscured the true focus of God's love. Gay and lesbian Christians, along with feminist theologians (who alert us to the unequal power relations that still shape many marriages), are beginning to develop a theology of friendship which could help the Church redeem the institution of marriage from harmful idolatry.

As a lesbian for whom the 'ideal' of marriage as the Christian relationship where God can be encountered most clearly is not an option, I have often reflected on the fact that Jesus of Nazareth, God incarnate, was either not married or if he was did not afford it any real prominence in his teaching. Indeed, Jesus called his followers away from their homes and spouses to follow him in building up the kingdom of God. Even a cursory reading of the Gospels reveals that the relationship which characterized Jesus' life and teaching was friendship. He came to proclaim the coming of God's reign on earth: the demolition of unequal power relations between people; all would be equal, rejoicing in their mutual interdependence. Jesus often used the image of a meal or banquet to convey what the kingdom would be like. Sharing a meal was an important and profound sign of friendship in his world. Jesus' whole mission was to convince those who gained power, comfort and status from creating elites and underclasses that such systems were contrary to the will of God and he had to convince those marginalized and oppressed by the socio-religious system that God was their friend. He called all into a recognition of their need for friendship and interdependence. Jesus built up around him a circle of friends who were to form the nucleus of the kingdom. These friendships cut across all social, religious and cultural barriers and undermined the whole religious and social structure of his day. In Jesus God comes among us not as master or king but as friend, as one of us, and transforms our lives by touching them with his friendship. He calls us to build up God's kingdom on earth by becoming friends with all.

In his teaching on divorce (*Mark 10:2-12*) Jesus overturns the Jewish law that understood the wife to be the property of the husband with no rights herself and allowed a man to divorce her easily. Jesus commanded the husband to treat the wife as an equal, as a friend, not as a piece of property that could be discarded. The Old Testament also teaches us that friendship is at the heart of God's will for creation. Genesis reveals that human beings are created to be in friendship with each other, God and the rest of creation. Man and woman are created equal - it is sin that corrupts that relationship into unequal power relations. God enters into a covenantal relationship with his people. Usually covenants were made between vassal and lord, victor and defeated, superior and dependent, but those who enter into a covenant relationship with God in the Hebrew Scriptures are referred to thereafter as God's 'friends' (*Exodus 33:11, Isaiah 41:8*) and the prophets confirm that God seeks a relationship with his people based upon mutual respect, love, justice and a recognition of interdependence, not upon domination, control and exploitation. This friendship will be reflected in the community's internal relationships. The prophets teach that human relationships must reflect the nature and quality of God's relationship with his people and it is significant that the two models provided by the Hebrew scriptures are not marriages but same-sex friendships - the friendship between David and Jonathan (described in highly erotic terms in the Hebrew) in *1 and 2 Samuel* and between Ruth and Naomi in the book of *Ruth*. Both relationships are cemented by a formal covenant pledge.

The doctrine of the Trinity also teaches us that friendship is the relationship that best illuminates the core of God's nature. God is imaged as a relationship of three equal persons bound together in mutuality and interdependence so that they can be described as one, yet their individuality and diversity is not dissolved but celebrated.

Lesbian and gay Christians are rediscovering what St Aelred of Rievaulx realized in the twelfth century,

> He is entirely alone who is without a friend. But what happiness, what security, what joy to have someone to whom you dare to speak on terms of equality as to another self;

> one to whom you can unblushingly make known what progress you have made in the spiritual life; one to whom you can entrust all the secrets of your heart ... What, therefore, is more pleasant than so to unite to oneself the spirit of another and of two to form one ... Whoever abides in friendship abides in God, and God in them ... God is friendship ... [4]

I think it is no coincidence that the Aelred, the first Christian theologian to develop a thorough and practical theology of friendship, was obviously sexually attracted to men.[5]

Many Christians are uncomfortable with the idea that friendship might include sexual expression of love. This is because early in its history Christianity absorbed from Greek culture a dualistic understanding of human nature. Human beings were thought to be made up of two separate entities - the body and the soul. The body was thought to be evil and constantly endangering the life of the soul which longed for release from the degenerate body and its sinful desires to ascend up to God. Just as the human being was dissected into two and ordered in a hierarchy so love was also dissected and ordered. The purest forms of love were agape (self-giving) and philia (friendship) because they were 'spiritual' loves involving no 'bodily' desire, unlike eros (self-fulfillment) and epithymia (sexual desire). It was this understanding of human nature and love that led the Church to idealize the celibate state at least until the Reformation. Yet this fear of the body and its desires has no basis in the Hebrew or Christian Scriptures. The God of the Old Testament is portrayed as a passionate lover by Hosea and all the other prophets testify that God's love for his people is not merely 'spiritual' it is expressed in very concrete, physical ways. In the story of Jesus of Nazareth we believe we see the story of God who saves not by loving us 'spiritually' from a distance but by coming among us in flesh and making his whole being completely vulnerable to us. The cross and the resurrection reveal that true friendship is profoundly passionate and embodied. The doctrines of the incarnation and resurrection blow dualism apart. As James Nelson has noted,

> Love is multidimensional. Each dimension needs the others for love's wholeness. Without eros, agape is cold and devoid of energizing passion. Without philia, epithymia becomes a sexual contract. Without epithymia, other ways of loving become bloodless. Without agape, the other dimensions of loving lose their self-giving, transformative power.[6]

St Aelred too knew that true friendship was a passionate, physical relationship and he encouraged the monks in his abbey to express their love for one another in a physical fashion although he drew the line at sexual expression because they had taken vows of celibacy. But his pre-monastic experience had taught him that friendship could be nurtured and celebrated through the mutual self-giving and affirmation of a sexual relationship and that this intimate physical expression of love was a sign and sacrament of the nature of God's love for us.

This is not to say however that it is appropriate for all friendships to be expressed in this uniquely intimate way. Although all relationships are capable of being sacramental (symbols and instruments of God's love) the act of sexual self-giving has the potential to be uniquely sacramental because of the complete and utter vulnerability of those involved. It is the vulnerability of God become human in a baby in Bethlehem or a God hanging naked on the cross. Such vulnerability, such complete and utter exposure of oneself, is only possible within the context of a relationship of deep mutual trust and knowledge, stability and security. I do not think it is usually possible for human beings to achieve such vulnerability in more than one relationship at a time, although many of my lesbian sisters, gay brothers and heterosexual friends would disagree. It is, of course, perfectly possible to make love without such vulnerability but I believe our sexuality is that which, in all of us, propels us to seek a relationship in which the depth of love makes such vulnerability a possibility and we will not be satisfied until we find it.

If friendship is the ideal Christian relationship then the only criteria the Churches should use to judge relationships is the quality of the friendship. This seems to be the thrust of Jesus' teaching in the parable of the sheep and the goats in *Matthew 25*. Marriage can then be defined as a relationship in which two friends of the opposite sex enter into a covenant of complete mutual vulnerability. The Church has always taught that husband and wife marry each other and the Christian community simply affirms that it recognises God's presence in the relationship and pledges its support and blessing in the wedding ceremony.

If friendship is the ideal Christian relationship then the Church should offer its blessing to same-sex friends who are seeking to incarnate their love for each other and God's love for them in a

friendship of committed vulnerability which could be thought of
as representing God's relationship with humanity. At the moment
such blessings are offered only informally and unofficially by a
few clergy and they very rarely take place at the beginning of a
gay and lesbian relationship. Gay and lesbian people tend to seek
a blessing only when they know their relationship to be blessed,
when they know that the vulerability they seek is possible with this
particular partner, that the friendship is strong and deep enough to
sustain it. In the light of the divorce rate among heterosexual
couples the gay and lesbian practice might be worth following.
The wedding ceremony would then become a celebration of a
relationship already obviously blessed and would lose its current
connotations of goods the wife) being transferred from one owner
(father) to another (husband) - connotations which are profoundly
antithetical to what should be the celebration of a friendship.
The elevation of friendship also offers us a fresh understanding of
celibacy. Celibacy can be understood as an alternative expression
of friendship. Celibates sacrifice the expression of friendship
through the complete vulerability of sexual intercourse in order to
enter into a friendship with a particular group of people. Celibates
are not bachelors or spinsters or hermits: they are people in
relationship and that relationship will be bodily and passionate as
all true friendships are. In sacrificing the one-to-one relationship
of complete vulnerability in order to commit themselves completely
to the building of a community, celibates could be said to represent
the sacrificial love of Christ for his friends.

Lesbian and gay Christians, having gone to their Churches asking
for bread, have often been turned away and sometimes a few
stones have been hurled after them. We have been forced to make
sense of our lives ourselves; we have been forced to do our own
theology. It is out of our experience that the theology of friendship
outlined above has developed. Although developed out of a very
particular and minority experience I believe it is truly inclusive in
that it offers the Church as a whole a new way of understanding
the increasingly beleagered institution of marriage and indeed the
equally beleagered celibate life as well. This 'new way' of
understanding is in fact rooted firmly in the Scriptures and Christ
event. It is time to pull down the idol. Too many lesbian and gay
and heterosexual people have been crushed in its service.
Friendship is something that is open to all of us, no matter what
our sexuality or gender. It is the truly inclusive, affirming and
empowering love that is the nature of God.

1   Homosexuality Working Party, *Homosexuality: A Christian view,* URC, 1991, p.6.

2   M. Scott Peck, *The Road Less Travelled,* Arrow, 1983, p.52.

3   It is important to remember, however, that many lesbian and gay people do get married, sometimes in an attempt to escape the reality of their homosexuality, sometimes because their homosexuality does not emegre until after marriage and sometimes because although predominantly homosexual they fall in love with a member of the opposite sex.

4   Aelred of Rievaulx, *De Spirituali Amicitia*

5   See John Boswell, *Christianity, Social Tolerance, and Homosexuality: Gay people in Western Europe from the beginning of the Christian era to the fourteenth century,* University of Chicago Press, 1980, pp.221-6. It is important to remember that 'homosexual' is a nineteenth century term and concept and therefore not a label Aelred would have applied to himself. However it is quite clear that he was emotionally and sexually orientated to men more than to women.

6   James Nelson, *The Intimate Connection: male sexuality, masculine spirituality,* SPCK, 1992, p.55.

Christians getting married:
The history of an institution

David M. Thompson

Many church people today would say that Christian marriage in
the twentieth century has come under threat in quite new ways. It
seems to be assumed that Christian marriage is a stable, relatively
unchanging institution, patterned on scripture. Today the stability
of marriage is threatened by the increased frequency of divorce
and a decline in sexual morality, often associated with the greater
availability of reliable contraceptives.

In fact, the story is much more complex than this. On the one
hand, it comes as a surprise to most people to learn than the church
marriage service as we know it was not obligatory for Christians
for the first thousand years of church history. On the other, it can
be argued that more people marry today than ever before, that more
of them have a real choice in the person whom they marry, that the
expectations of personal fulfilment that married people have are
much greater, and that the average length of a marriage is much
greater than at any time in the past. One historian has written that
'it looks very much as if modern divorce is simply a functional
substitute for death'.[1] Standards of sexual morality are probably
no lower today than they were at the end of the eighteenth century:
indeed the assumption today that men in positions of public
leadership will not normally have mistresses is not only a break
with the eighteenth century but even with that great age of morality
– the Victorian era.

Clearly this is an over-simple statement of the case on both sides,
but the important point is that the history of Christian marriage
cannot be understood as a simple story of progress or decay.
There are movements, sometimes dramatic movements, but they
move in both, or even all, directions. Nor is there any reason to
suppose that this situation is likely to change. Twentieth-century
awareness of the multi-cultural nature of the world has also made
us aware that marriage, including Christian marriage, is differently
understood in different cultures. It is no longer possible to treat
the history of Christian marriage simply from the standpoint of
Western Christendom; and in any case the English (as distinct from

the Scottish) experience of marriage is almost unique in the West for reasons which are too complex to be discussed adequately here.

Nevertheless the point of this essay is to sketch the background to the contemporary British scene. It therefore begins with a brief account of the development of Christian marriage in both East and West, with particular attention to the way in which the particular circumstances of the English Reformation affected its development in England. The changes in the law in the nineteenth and twentieth centuries will be explained so as to illuminate the present position, particularly as it affects the United Reformed Church. Then a series of issues which recur through the history will be examined in a little more detail. Finally, we shall try to see whether any common threads emerge which enable us to answer the question, What is Christian marriage?

Obviously marriage is not a uniquely Christian institution. Indeed most of the things we associate with weddings have nothing to do with Christianity at all. The giving away of the bride by her father, her white dress and veil, the flowers, the joining of hands and the wedding cake all come from Roman tradition; the engagement ring is Eastern in origin, and reached the West by way of Spain; the wedding ring is Germanic; and the blessing of the rings is peculiar to the British Isles.[2] By definition the earliest married members of the Church approached marriage with pre-Christian assumptions. Initially these were Jewish, but from an early point and to an increasing extent they were Gentile. Indeed the relatively rapid marginalization of Jewish Christians meant that the marriage norms which Christianity inherited were more Roman than Jewish. This can be seen even in the earliest gospel – Mark – where Jesus is represented as referring to the possibility of a wife divorcing her husband which was impossible in contemporary Jewish law (*Mark 10:11-12*), suggesting that it may be a reflection of the Gentile environment of the church for which the gospel was written.[3] Most pagan converts were probably married when they became Christians, so the idea of a church marriage as distinct from marriage in the traditional family setting did not arise. The *Epistle to Diognetus* suggests that Christian marriages were much the same as pagan marriages, and the Synod of Elvira (c 306) accepted this as normal. The earliest evidence of a liturgical celebration of marriage in Rome, and Italy more generally, is from the fourth century: such liturgical solemnisation was only available for first marriages and it was obligatory only for the lower clergy before

43

the eleventh century.[4] Even more interesting is the fact that such religious ceremonies as did take place were not regarded as essential to the validity of the marriage as late as the ninth century: what was necessary was the mutual consent of the partners.[5]

When the Roman Empire adopted Christianity as its official religion, the civil law of marriage was modified in a Christian direction to some extent, though differences still remained. For the Eastern Churches the Quinisext Council of Trullo (692) marked a turning point, though it was only partly accepted by the Church of Rome. The Council ruled that priests and deacons were not debarred from marriage, though it was forbidden after ordination: bishops, however, were forbidden to live with their wives, who had to retire to a suitably distant monastery. (The third canon of the Council of Nicaea in 325 had forbidden women other than mothers, sisters or aunts to live with bishops, priests and deacons.)[6] By the end of the ninth century the Eastern Empire ruled that only marriages blessed by the Church should count as legitimate, and this provision, at least in relation to Christian subjects, survived when the Ottoman Empire replaced the Eastern Empire in the fifteenth century. The church in the East was therefore given control of marriage by the state, something which has never happened in quite that way in the West. On the other hand, the permission for divorce which was part of the Emperor Justinian's civil law, was also accepted by the Eastern Church.[7]

In the West the situation was complicated by the breakdown of the Empire under the barbarian invasions. In one sense this made it easier for the Church to impose its own marriage rules because of the lack of a coherent secular power; in another it made it more difficult because the Church now encountered a much greater variety of marriage customs in the newly evangelised European territories north and west of the Alps. For example, the Germanic tribes were hostile to the consent theory of marriage, because they still saw it essentially as a contract between two tribes or families. Schillebeeckx writes that, 'the Celts and Anglo-Saxons originally regarded the woman simply as merchandise, and marriages consequently above all as a sort of deed of purchase or conveyance'.[8] The Western Church did not have a code of canon law equivalent to the Eastern Code of 883 (itself an elaboration of John the Scholastics Nomocanon of 565) until Gratian's *Decretum* of 1140. In the ninth century strenuous efforts were made by the Church to gain control of marriage but they failed, and in practice the Church accepted the legislative and judicial power of the state in matrimonial affairs.

From the tenth to the twelfth century a campaign of reform was waged which eventually influenced the papacy itself. This campaign had two main features: the drive to secure clerical celibacy, and a concern to make marriages public (since this simplified the handling of subsequent legal disputes over whether a marriage had taken place). In the fourth century when Augustine grew up it was not uncommon for men to live with concubines: a Spanish synod of 400 decreed that if a man was faithful to his concubine as if she was a wife, there was no bar to communion.[9] Augustine himself, before his conversion, had a concubine for several years, by whom he had a son, until his mother decided that he should be married and his mistress was 'torn from my side as an impediment to my marriage'.[10] In the late eleventh century and early twelfth century the secular canons of several English cathedrals were married, and their children succeeded them in their canonries, notably at St Paul's. This was also the period when Heloise illegally but validly married Peter Abelard, while she was living with her uncle who was a canon of Notre Dame in Paris, though their marriage was subsequently dissolved and both embraced the monastic life.[11] The Lateran Councils of 1123, 1139, 1179 and 1215 were all concerned with clerical reform in various ways. Each of them emphasised that the clergy should be celibate; and there is some evidence to suggest that they were successful in achieving that. The Church also campaigned to make marriages public: this is the time when marriage ceremonies began to move from the home to the church porch, though many were still conducted at home in the fifteenth century in England.[12] The culmination of the Church's attack on clandestine marriages came at 24th session of the Council of Trent in 1563, which required the presence of a priest and other witnesses at a wedding, and therefore seemed to imply that in some way a priest made a marriage a departure from the traditional view that marriage was made by the partners themselves. Trent also consolidated the teaching on the sacramental character of marriage and the scholastic notion of its indissolubility, which had been developing since the twelfth century.[13]

By this time, however, the Protestant Reformation had taken place and this led to a movement in the opposite direction. For different reasons Lutherans and Calvinists were inclined to leave marriage to be regulated by the state alone. Marriage was not regarded as a sacrament; and divorce, where it was allowed, was regarded as dissolving marriage completely. The consequences of this can be seen in Scotland where the post-Reformation law on marriage and divorce was more liberal than that in England. The *First Book of Discipline* of 1560 laid down that marriage should be public, before the congregation in church after the proclamation of banns: divorce was permitted on grounds of adultery and, after 1573, desertion. In other words the essential basis of marriage rested on the consent of the parties and the presence of witnesses.[14] The English Reformation, of course, was peculiarly entwined with problems of the law of marriage because of Henry VIII's need for an heir. The result was that the medieval position survived, except that the papal power of providing dispensations was excluded. But there was no new civil legislation on marriage until 1753, when in an effort to eliminate clandestine marriages it was enacted that (apart from Jews and Quakers) the only legally recognized marriages in England would be those conducted by Anglican clergymen in the parish church of one of the partners.

However, as the exceptions noted make clear, the situation was complicated by the existence of religious dissent. After the Great Ejection of 1662 Protestant nonconformists had won a measure of toleration in 1689. But the new legislation put fresh pressure on them. By the early nineteenth century nonconformists were backing the campaign for civil registration of births, marriages and deaths, an objective achieved in 1836. An Act of 1834 made it possible for ministers of other churches than the Church of Scotland and the Episcopal Church of Scotland to celebrate marriages north of the border.

The Marriage Act of 1836 made legal marriage possible outside the Church of England, but it did not make nonconformist marriage services legal. The declarations made by both partners that there is no legal impediment to their marriage and that they take each other to be husband and wife had to be made in the form specified by statute and in the presence of a civil registrar, who was also the local officer in charge of the administration of the Poor Law. Only in 1898 was the present system introduced, whereby other persons (usually, but not necessarily, ministers) could be authorised to hear the declarations. This made it possible to integrate the legally required declarations with the rest of the marriage service. These 'authorised persons' have the duty and authority to register the marriage, and the Marriage Act of 1949 consolidated the legislation on this point. It is worth noting in passing that England remains different from those countries in which a civil marriage ceremony is compulsory and the church service in effect blesses a marriage that has already legally taken place (though, because of the delicacies of the compromise in church-state relations involved, a careful veil of ambiguity is usually drawn over this point).

In Britain since the nineteenth century discussion about marriage has been largely prompted by the question of divorce. The English Reformation by abolishing dispensations had left no way apart from statute for the termination of marriages. After 1660 a relatively small number of people succeeded in obtaining private divorce bills from parliament, though this was necessarily expensive. For the mass of ordinary people *de facto* separation, desertion or the traditional wife sale (immortalised in Thomas Hardy's *The Mayor of Casterbridge*) were the only alternatives to straightforward bigamy. In 1857 a Divorce Law was passed to make it possible for the courts to dissolve the marriage of a husband who proved his wife was guilty of adultery: until 1923 a wife had to prove her husband guilty of cruelty as well as adultery. In 1937 Sir Alan Herbert, an Independent Member of Parliament who had secured election for Oxford University largely on this issue, succeeded in carrying through a Private Member's Bill to extend the grounds for divorce, opening up for the first time a gap between the grounds acknowledged as legitimate by the Church of England and those approved by the state. The state also came to recognise and provide for legal separations.

In 1969 the situation was changed completely when a new Divorce Law removed the concept of the matrimonial offence, and made the sole ground for divorce the 'irretrievable breakdown' of marriage. Although strenuous efforts were made to avoid the impression that this meant the introduction of divorce by consent, the fact that marriages could be dissolved if the partners had lived apart by consent for two years, or without the consent of one partner for five years, made it difficult to see the distinction in practice. After 1971 the number of divorces rose dramatically – from 25,000 in 1970 to 121,000 by 1975; though it is always possible to ask how far this recognizes publicly what had for a considerable time been the case privately. Moreover, procedural changes introduced between 1973 and 1977 to make it possible to secure divorces by affidavit rather than attendance at court made divorce even easier to obtain than had originally been intended.[15] Indeed it can also be argued that the availability of legal aid has been much more significant in giving the majority of people access to divorce than the substantive legislation itself.

This sketch has shown that the history of marriage is not a simple one; but several issues recur constantly. A fundamental one is monogamy. The patriarchs and kings of the Old Testament often had more than one wife, though polygamy was rare by the time of Jesus. But it is clear that the prohibition on adultery and the requirement for faithfulness in marriage in the Old Testament do not completely exclude polygamy, though the Genesis passage about male and female becoming one flesh both by its date and content probably indicates the movement towards monogamy. Obviously polygamy was mainly for the rich and powerful. This was not an issue for most of the first 1500 years of the Church's history, but it has arisen more directly with the missionary movement to non-European peoples, and has been very controversial.

However, there is a more subtle question, which can easily be overlooked. Does monogamy mean that one should only have one husband or wife ever, rather than at any one time? The trick question put to Jesus in the Gospels[16] in this matter is well known, and typically Jesus did not answer it. His statement that after the resurrection of the dead 'they neither marry nor are given in marriage' implies that marriage is essentially a temporal phenomenon, and is supported by Paul's statement in *Romans 7:2* that a woman is bound to her husband only so long as he lives. A similar comment in *1 Corinthians 7:39* is supplemented by Paul's own view that he thinks it is better if she does not remarry and a characteristically frank statement that he thinks he has the Spirit of God. What is interesting about that, however, is that it raises the question of whether Paul knew of Jesus's statement in *Mark* or whether the words attributed to Jesus are in fact later additions.[17] But the issue has remained to vex Christian scholars, particularly when they reflect on the eternal nature of the marriage relationship. Is marriage essentially a temporal phenomenon? One only has to talk to bereaved partners in marriage to see how much the prospect of reunion after death can mean to them. Yet equally in talking to widowed persons who have remarried one can see how much their second marriage means to them.

We are thus brought very quickly into the area of the biblical teaching on marriage. Is there a single biblical view of marriage? What is the relationship between the biblical view(s) and the/a Christian view? The sharpest way in which that point can be put is this: does it make sense to treat writings which are given canonical status because of the witness they bear to the saving acts of God, particularly in the death and resurrection of Jesus Christ, as though everything they contain, whether or not it is related to the saving acts of God, is to be regarded as divinely inspired teaching? Schillebeeckx has shown very clearly the different layers of meaning attached to marriage in the Old Testament. The teaching of Jesus is usually regarded as central, but what exactly was Jesus's teaching? Apart from biblical critical questions concerning authenticity, there is the important point noted by Hugh Montefiore in the 1971 Church of England report that it is uncertain whether Jesus's teaching should be regarded as *halakah* legal prescriptions for conduct or *haggadah* religious truths tellingly illustrated by extreme statements which are not necessarily intended to be taken literally, or possibly neither.[18] The comments on marriage in *Ephesians 5* increase what is at stake by seeing marriage as the figure of the relationship between Christ and the Church: but is this intended to help us understand the nature of the Church or the nature of marriage?

An immediately related question is the relation of marriage to sex and procreation. Nowadays there is a strong reaction against the view that marriage is 'a remedy against sin',[19] and such language has generally been eliminated from modern marriage liturgies. The significance of mutual love and consent, which has a long history, is stressed. Even the procreation of children is not now given as the primary purpose of marriage in modern Protestant services. John Hunter's *Devotional Services for Public Worship* (1880), which was quite popular among Congregationalists, did not refer to it at all; and in the service books of the Congregational Union and the Presbyterian Church of England the reference to the procreation of children in the statement on the purpose of marriage was bracketed, so that it could be omitted in cases where it was not relevant (as it was in the first *Book of Services* published by the United Reformed Church in 1980). However, in the new Roman Catholic canon law, although canon 1055 states that the marriage covenant is ordered to the well being of the spouses and to the procreation and upbringing of children, later canons, (e.g. 1084, 1096) give a greater priority to procreation in determining the validity of marriage.[20] This illustrates the fact that for much of its history the Church has had a 'hang up' about sex. In large part this is due to the legacy of Augustine who, after renouncing his early life, came to regard sexual intercourse itself as the means by which original sin was passed from one generation to the next. At certain periods teaching about marriage has been used to demean the position of women and to reinforce patriarchal notions. Some feminists have argued that these notions are inextricably entangled with Christianity; others, while not going so far, have wanted to modify Christian teaching significantly to remove what they regard as patriarchal remnants.[21] How can such questions be resolved? Great medical changes have taken place in our own day improving the safety of childbirth and facilitating reliable contraception. As a result the concern to ensure the survival of the family or species has been replaced by an anxiety about the sustainability of continued population growth. So we feel we are in a new situation, scarcely envisaged in biblical times in which sexual relations cease to be inextricably entwined with procreation. Actually that situation is not as new as we sometimes imagine, since the knowledge of certain methods of avoiding conception goes back at least as far as the ancient Greeks. The extent to which we are willing to consider rethinking some of these questions will depend on how far we regard biblical and church teaching through the ages as conditioned by temporal circumstances as well as by the will of God.

Another related question is that of celibacy or virginity. Can these states be advocated without there being implicit value judgements between celibacy and married status? Does a celibate person always have a more inclusive commitment to others than a married person? Must the exclusivity of marriage always be some kind of barrier to openness? One of the interesting things which emerges from the history of the marriage liturgy is that from the fourth century onwards the ceremonies for the veiling of a bride and the veiling of a virgin were self-consciously parallel, since in each case the governing image was the marriage between Christ and the Church. The Taize brother, Max Thurian, has argued that 'when the vocation of celibacy is underrated, so is that of marriage'.[22] Similarly the Anglican scholar, A.M. Allchin, writing about the Eastern Orthodox view of marriage, remarked that 'once maturity, integrity of love is defined as the end of marriage, then its relation to the call to celibacy at once becomes clearer. It is in love that we become persons; love for God, and love for one another. The fullness of that love is the goal of both ways'.[23] Thus a Greek scholar can criticise Western views of marriage and monasticism as being too utilitarian, too concerned with the purpose of the vocation rather than the vocation itself. True marriage involves the transformation of selfish passion between two individuals into a free, responsible relationship of love between two persons, something which can only become possible as human 'perverse and wayward loves are redirected and purified through the love of a crucified and risen God'.[24]

How important then is love? Or more precisely, how important is love before marriage? We have grown so used to the idea that love is a prerequisite that we look upon arranged marriages with horror. But for most of human history the pattern has been that husband and wife learned to love each other after their marriage, rather than before. In an important sense that is still true, for few married couples could honestly say that their initial love had been sufficient to carry them through. Professor Schillebeeckx is also probably right to remind us that the nature of the medieval evidence may tend to understate the extent of marital love in that period, just as a survey of twentieth-century films would understate it today.[25] Nevertheless there is perhaps today a danger of marriage becoming too individualistic. The traditional social implications of marriage, especially for the legitimacy of children and the inheritance of property, are no longer the exclusive concerns of the wealthy. In a property-owning democracy, and even in a welfare state, these concerns affect all apart from the most marginalised. This is why the state cannot be indifferent to marriage. Reformed Christians have historically rejected the view that marriage is exclusively the concern of the Church, but since the Church has a particular teaching about the nature of Christian marriage the Reformed position involves an ongoing dialogue between church and state about their respective roles in marriage.

This is one reason why the question of the sacramental character of marriage is important. The theory that there are seven sacraments emerged in the Western Church in the twelfth century; and it is significant that marriage was regarded as one of them, in view of its associations with sex, property settlements etc. The immediate origin of this lies in the Vulgate's rendering of the Greek *mysterion* in *Ephesians 5:32* ('This is a great mystery, and I am applying it to Christ and the church') as *sacramentum*. It seems likely that the canon lawyers understanding of *sacramentum* as involving indissolubility was initially more important than any theology of marriage as an effective sign of grace.[26] The Reformers argued that marriage was part of the order of nature rather than grace, and therefore that to link it with baptism and communion was confusing, a position still echoed by the Church of England's 1971 report: marriage belongs to the order of creation rather than that of redemption.[27] The Council of Trent defined marriage as a sacrament in 1563, but did not really explain the theological basis for this. Moreover the fact that the sacramental character of marriage was so closely tied to the notion of its indissolubility has not proved helpful to subsequent theological reflection. A contemporary Roman Catholic writer expresses the dilemma thus: 'Priests find themselves torn between a legal demand which normally leads them to bless in church the marriage of all those baptized persons who ask for it and a pastoral sense which moves them to confer the sacrament only on those who want really to live out their union in the perspective of Christian faith.'[28] Reformed Christians can more easily affirm a sacramental character for marriage than see it in itself as a sacrament. Moreover, without minimizing the extent to which God's grace can break through into the most unlikely situations in ways which are completely unpredictable, the historian of marriage is bound to observe that there is only sketchy evidence for the view that the mass of the population in Europe have ever really accepted the full theological implications of Christian marriage. When civil marriage was made possible in England in 1836 it rapidly became popular in certain parts of the country in ways which do not simply correlate with the presence of nonconformity but almost suggest an older tradition, temporarily obscured by the legislation of 1753.[29]

This brings us back to the fundamental question of what a theological reflection on marriage involves. Are we concerned with the theological interpretation of something which is natural, or is there something qualitatively different in the marriage of two Christians? If so, is that empirically observable or is it a matter of faith? John Bowker points out that in the Jewish and Christian tradition God is believed to give meaning to things rather than things giving meaning to God or even being identified with God.[30] In this way the biblical statement that 'a man leaves his father and his mother and clings to his wife, and they become one flesh' (*Genesis 2:24*) takes the secular fact of marriage and gives it divine significance by relating it to the creation. The characterization of marriage in terms of the relationship between Christ and his church in *Ephesians* performs a similar function in the New Testament.

Thus Professor Schillebeeckx can describe marriage as 'a secular reality which has entered salvation', and go on to say that 'this definitive surrender to another person, without any foreknowledge of what may happen in the future, is the human manifestation of man's definitive surrender to the other being, God'.[31] At one level marriages between Christians are no different from those of anybody else, but Christians have a particular understanding of what is involved in marriage as a calling.

It is significant that the 1989 *Service Book* of the United Reformed Church emphasises that marriage is given by God:

> Marriage is a gift and calling of God, and is not to be entered upon lightly or thoughtlessly, but reverently and responsibly, in obedience to the gospel of Christ. God has given us marriage so that husband and wife may find comfort and companionship in each other and live faithfully together for the whole of their lives. God has given us marriage so that husband and wife may love and honour each other, enrich and encourage each other, and know each other with tenderness and joy. God has given us marriage for the birth and nurture of children, so that they may grow up in the security of love, and come to experience the freedom of faith. God has given us marriage so that husband and wife, being joined together as Christ with his Church, may be a sign of unity and mutual commitment, for the enrichment of society and the strengthening of community.[32]

Even if Reformed Christians would still hesitate to call marriage a sacrament as such, they would understand A.M. Allchin's comment that 'marriage may be seen as a sacrament in two principal ways: first, as an image and reflection of the great sacrament of Christ and the Church; then as one of the gifts and callings within the Church which goes to make up the life of the whole community'.[33] They would warm to Fr Bagot's affirmation that the essence of marriage is 'to live out love as Christ lived it', and further that 'love lived in God creates an eternal bond...a paradoxical truth which is both crucifying and the source of life'.[34] They are moved by the Old Testament picture in the book of *Hosea* where the prophet's continuing love for his faithless wife, Gomer, becomes a way of expressing the profound truth that God will not cast off Israel. Yet they prefer the patristic emphasis on the morally binding nature of marriage to the scholastic proposition that it is ontologically indissoluble; and they are particularly concerned that too often the practical problems of divorce have been allowed to set the agenda for the understanding of marriage. Consequently they sympathise with John Bowker's observation that 'the apparent conflict between the intention of marriage and remarriage after divorce reflects the contrast between the fact of failure and the fact of redemption'.[35] For redemption - the redemption of sinful human beings - lies at the heart of Reformed theology.

Are there then any common threads running through this story? When a local United Reformed congregation celebrates a marriage, it celebrates the free commitment and mutual exchange of promises between two people, sharing their joy, and praying for God's blessing upon them. The prayers include a prayer that the couple 'in repentance and in faith' may know God 'as a God of mercy and new beginnings, who forgives our failures, restores our wholeness, and renews our hope'.[36] Behind that lies a long history which draws on many traditions. At the heart of it there is an ongoing community in at least three ways: the community of husband and wife, the human community to which they belong, and the community of that people with their God.

1   L. Stone, *The Family, Sex and Marriage in England, 1500-1800,* Penguin 1979, 46.
2   E. Schillebeeckx, *Marriage: human reality and saving mystery,* Sheed & Ward 1976, 235, 240, 242, 257, 259, 266.
3   See *Marriage, Divorce and the Church,* SPCK 1971, 82-3.
4   Schillebeeckx, *Marriage,* 233, 262.
5   T.A. Lacey & R.C. Mortimer, *Marriage in Church and State,* SPCK 1947, 40-2.
6   N.P. Tanner ed), *Decrees of the Ecumenical Councils,* Sheed & Ward 1990, i, 7.
7   Lacey & Mortimer, *Marriage in Church and state,* 102-9.
8   Schillebeeckx, *Marriage,* 256, 260.
9   H. Chadwick, *The Early Church,* Penguin 1967, 217.
10 Augustine, *Confessions,* iv, 2; vi, 23, 25, ed. A.C. Outler, SCM 1955, 77, 130-1, 132.
11 C.N.L. Brooke, *The Medieval Idea of Marriage,* Oxford University Press 1989, 82-92, 105-8.
12 Brooke, *The Medieval Idea of Marriage,* 248-57.
13 For the decree 'Tametsi' of the Council of Trent, see Tanner, *Decrees of the Ecumenical Councils,* ii, 755-9.
14 K.M. Boyd, *Scottish Church attitudes to Sex, Marriage and the Family 1850-1914,* John Donald 1980, 48-9.
15 P.A. Welsby, *A History of the Church of England, 1945-1980,* Oxford University Press 1984, 228-9.
16 Mark 12:18-27 and parallels.

17 Much depends here on what one is looking for in the passage: most concentrate on the implication that divorce is not possible and another common theme is the significance of celibacy, cf. *Marriage, Divorce and the Church,* 89-90; Schillebeeckx, *Marriage,* 121-2.

18 *Marriage, Divorce and the Church,* 92-5.

19 As stated, for example, in the preface to the Marriage Service in the *Book of Common Prayer* of 1662. Similarly the Homily on 'The State of Matrimony' 1562) states in the second sentence that marriage was instituted 'to the intent that man and woman should live lawfully in a perpetual friendly fellowship, to bring forth fruit, and to avoid fornication: by which means a good conscience might be preserved on both parties in bridling the corrupt inclinations of the flesh within the limits of honesty': *Certain Sermons or Homilies appointed to be read in Churches,* SPCK 1938, 534.

20 *The Code of Canon Law* English translation), Collins 1983, 189, 193, 195.

21 For a critical history of the Church's attitude to sexuality see U. Ranke-Heinemann, *Eunochs for the Kingdom of Heaven,* Penguin 1991.

22 Schillebeeckx, *Marriage,* 306-12: the quotation from M. Thurian, *Marriage and Celibacy,* Allenson 1959, is on p 312.

23 *Marriage, Divorce and the Church,* 115.

24 *Ibid,* 117.

25 Schillebeeckx, *Marriage,* xxiv.

26 *Ibid,* 328-32.

27 *Marriage, Divorce and the Church,* 37.

28 J-P. Bagot, *How to Understand Marriage,* SCM Press 1987, 58.

29 0. Anderson, 'The Incidence of Civil Marriage in Victorian England and Wales', *Past and Present,* 69 1975), 50-87.

30 *Marriage, Divorce and the Church,* 100.

31 Schillebeeckx, *Marriage,* 194, 206, 207.

32 Service Book, Oxford University Press 1989, 51-52. The language is not greatly altered from the first *Book of Services* of the United Reformed Church St Andrew's Press 1980) 69.

33 *Marriage, Divorce and the Church,* 118.

34 Bagot, *How to Understand Marriage,* 66, 72.

35 *Marriage, Divorce and the Church,* 105.

36 *Service Book,* 53.

Something of concern to God

David Cockerell

A funeral demands special clothes and carriage, very considerable
expense, and to attend such an event, second cousins will take a
day off work, and think it but dutifully spent. Yet a marriage is, by
comparison, almost unnoticed. ... It occurs most frequently on a
Saturday or Sunday, as it is hardly worthwhile to lose a day's work
... few attend it outside a small circle of lady friends.

That account, written in 1911, offers a perhaps surprising contrast
with the situation we are familiar with today. Now a wedding
too demands special clothes and carriage, and certainly a very
considerable expense. But then a marriage in 1911 was no fairy-
tale fantasy. For many young women it represented perhaps the
only escape from the drudgery of the factory or service; but almost
certainly more drudgery, and perhaps too acute poverty, followed.
Gareth Stedman Jones remarks that 'among all sectors of the
working class, marriage meant children and the constant drudgery
of work on a declining standard of living until they were old
enough to bring money into the home'.[1] Nonetheless, girls actively
sought marriage, often in their teens, and the unmarried woman
became something of a curiosity and even a music-hall joke as in
the song:

> Why am I always the bridesmaid,
> Never the blushing bride?
> Ding! Dong! Wedding bells
> Only ring for other girls ...

But such derisory attitudes towards unmarried women – so that
the word 'spinster' took on pejorative overtones of failure and
dowdiness – were not restricted to working-class women.
Alasdair MacIntyre says that

> when production was within the household the unmarried
> sister or aunt was a useful and valued member of the
> household; the "spinster", not surprisingly, did the spinning.
> It is only at the beginning of the eighteenth century that the
> expression becomes denigratory; it is only then that the
> woman who does not marry has to fear expulsion into drudgery
> as her characteristic lot. Hence to refuse even a bad marriage
> is an act of great courage.[2]

Notice the prevalence of the word 'drudgery' here. Women faced a choice between the drudgery and failure of spinsterhood on the one hand or the drudgery and poverty of child-rearing on the other. As MacIntyre suggests, this situation reflects a growing dualism between the workplace and the home, and, with it, an increasingly rigid demarcation of roles as between the sexes. As the home became the place of relaxation and leisure, so 'wives increasingly retreated from productive employment itself except in the form of home work. Home and family life tended to become a depoliticised haven.'[3] In this 'haven', however, the wife was expected to rule and to be the decision-maker, often with the husband being treated as little more than a lodger – 'only entrusted with pocket money to be spent on fares, beer, tobacco and a trades union or club subscription.'[4] The same dualism affected middle-class women too, though here it was dealt with in a different way: here, as Alasdair MacIntyre remarks, 'occupations have to be invented – fine needlework, the reading of bad novels and organised opportunities for gossip, which are then thought of by both men and women as "essentially feminine".'[5] Incarceration in the home, whether with the latest three-volume novel or the latest babies and toddlers for company, does not bring out the best in people; a contemporary feminist writer comments upon its effects:

> It produces a tendency to small-mindedness, petty jealousy, irrational emotionality and random violence, dependency, complete selfishness and possessiveness, passivity, a lack of vision and conservatism.[6]

- which then come to be identified as 'essentially feminine' traits. Maud Pember Reeves' famous study of working class family life in 1911, *Round About A Pound A Week,* records a typical story:

> Mrs O knows nothing of her neighbours, and, until the visitor insisted on the children's getting out every afternoon, and agitated for the boots, Mrs O never took them out. She did her shopping at night in order that her old slippers might not be seen. She sat indoors and mended and made clothes in her neat room, while her pale little girl amused herself as best she could and the baby slept on the bed. The husband merely ate and slept at home … [7]

In contrast with all of this, the largely male-dominated churches were at the same time constructing a highly idealised picture of the home and family life – the preservation of which has come to seem to many to be one of the principal public functions of the Church. This meshed not only with the dualism I have noted, in which the churches found themselves on the home/family/leisure/female side, but also with an idealised view of women and childbearing (often combined in practice with a negative and defensive attitude towards real women) which found expression in the Anglo-Catholic movement's devotion to a fantasised Mary. Motherhood – Mother Church – Mary Mother of Jesus, made a powerful rhetorical triangle which could be used to instil a sense of guilt and failure in real women who could never reach the ideal of passive and joyful service demonstrated by Mary towards the male God/husband through her sexless conception of Jesus.

It is now quite frequently pointed out how the Church reinforces its idealisation of the nuclear family through its use of family typology and the emphasis on 'family services'; and its hostility towards alternative domestic and sexual practices.[8] For instance, the Church of England report *Children in the Way* (about the place of children in the church) quotes a letter to the Methodist Recorder:

> The trouble with using 'family' as an image for the church (apart from the fact that every time I hear it I feel like a pacifist hearing the church referred to as 'God's Army') is that it implies that family life is superior to all other ways of life, an idea which has no support in the Gospel. (*p.32*)

The report goes on to comment upon 'the potential pain and sense of exclusion for those who are widowed and those whose marriages are broken; or the difficulties and conflicts of loyalties for those whose partners are indifferent or hostile to the church.' But that correspondent to the Methodist Recorder surely hits on the main point. The New Testament essays a number of models for understanding the Church; indeed, it is more pluralistic in this regard than we might at first think. But 'family' isn't one of them. The nearest is the injunction (which comes from the same chapter as the reading set in the ASB lectionary for the 14th Sunday after Pentecost – theme 'The Family') that 'the man is the head of the woman, just as Christ is also the head of the church' (*Ephesians 5.22-23*) – hardly, we might feel, a very helpful image for understanding either the church or the family today. American research has suggested[9] that women who believe that their subordination to men is sanctioned by scripture may have particular conflicts of loyalty if they are abused by their husbands, so that much abuse of women in Christian families goes unreported; and is in any case unlikely to be acknowledged by churches which retain an ideological commitment to the sanctity of the 'Christian family'. Research into problems within clergy marriages[10] likewise suggests a process of denial and repression due to a perceived need to protect 'the family' in the church as well as 'of' the Church. This can leave church-people at least bewildered, at worst hostile and unsupportive, when the marriages of clergy or leading lay people run into trouble – or, indeed, when they 'come out' as gay. Instead of being supported and helped at a time of pain and difficulty, such unfortunate people often experience pain and rejection from the church 'family', an institution which is in practice often very poorly equipped for dealing with anomalies and deviances. The notion of 'family' here threatens to become a code-word for an ideology which binds church-people together around a highly specific, and exclusive, set of social mores.

The relationship between sex, marriage and the Church has an interesting and complex history, and in what follows I am drawing upon Alan MacFarlane's study, *Marriage and Love in England 1300-1840.*[11] Our act of marriage was originally a two-stage process, which began with betrothal. This was, effectively, the 'marriage', and it was sexually consummated; it required no ecclesiastical or religious validation.

> Later, a public celebration and announcement of the wedding might take place – the "gift", the "bridal", or "nuptials", as it became known. This was the occasion when friends and relatives assembled to feast and hear the financial details (*p.310*).

For the first of these, MacFarlane stresses, 'there was no necessity for a clergyman to be present, or for any religious ceremony'. By the end of the sixteenth century, a church service remained an optional extra, 'lending gravity to the occasion', but secondary to more secular, and often more sexually explicit, celebrations. Many people avoided the publicity of the church service, with its 'immodest' calling of banns. Thus 'in the seventeenth and early eighteenth centuries it was common for couples to confirm their prenuptial arrangements through clandestine marriages. These were performed, without the publicity of banns, at irregular times and in irregular places – not only by laymen but also by impoverished clergy who for a small fee would preside over vows which canon law regarded as being equivalent to a church

marriage.'[12] The most famous area for these 'little weddings' was
around the Fleet in London, and they also had the advantages of
avoiding parental interference and the expense of an elaborate
wedding-feast. In an attempt to regulate what was becoming a
chaotic state of affairs, the Hardwicke Act of 1753 abolished all
but church weddings. John Gillis comments, 'The propertied
elites had already begun to distinguish sharply between the
engaged and the married. In polite circles an affianced couple no
longer had the legal and sexual rights previously assigned to the
betrothed. With the 1753 Act these groups imposed their norms on
the rest of the population.'[13] This imposition clearly did much to
support the Church's social power and its control over the lives of
ordinary people.

At the same time, the Church was developing a view of marriage
as 'something of concern to God', in MacFarlane's words. Quite
what that was was always harder to define. Thus the preface to the
marriage service in the *Book of Common Prayer* (1662) strains to
bring into service Paul's sexual analogy for the relation between
Christ and the church, supported rather unconvincingly by a
reference to Jesus' presence at the marriage at Cana. At a time
when sexual abstinence was still widely regarded as a mark of
the Christian life, the Prayer Book showed its true colours, and
concerns, in its desire to control 'men's carnal lusts and appetites,
like brute beasts that have no understanding'. The idea of sexuality
as inherently 'bestial', somehow subhuman, is an important
ingredient in a view of marriage as 'ordained for a remedy against
sin, and to avoid fornication; that such persons as have not the gift
of continency might marry, and keep themselves undefiled members
of Christ's body'. Sex is seen here in grudging and negative terms:
the real gift is 'continency' and marriage, far from a joyful and
positive institution, is seen as a divinely sanctioned brake on 'carnal
lusts' which, left unchecked, would lead to sin and fornication. The
reference to Christ's body is, we feel, little more than a theological
ornament.

A prurient desire to control people's lives, including their sex
lives, has always been one of the less attractive features of English
Christianity, and here it combines with a negative and guilt-
inducing view of sex and a craving for respectability, especially
among the rising middle class, to create a powerful engine to drive
the church's teaching on the family. What is equally remarkable,
whether we consult the seventeenth or the twentieth-century prayer

books, is how thin and frankly unconvincing the skein of theology is which wraps this package.

The sense of strain is heightened if we consider further the contrast between ecclesiastical convention and the life and ministry of Jesus. A striking and inescapable aspect of Jesus' life is that he remained unmarried, and this was clearly a prophetic sign. The Son of Man had to have nowhere to lay his head, to be free to move among his people, challenging them and calling them on in the name of God's kingdom. Jesus' teaching about the family is scandalously subversive: 'If anyone come to me and does not hate his own father and mother and wife and children and brothers and sisters, yes, and even his own life, he cannot be my disciple.' (*Luke 14.26*) There could scarcely be a stronger denunciation of the family, except perhaps this: 'I have come to set a man against his father, and a daughter against her mother, and a daughter-in-law against her mother-in-law; and a man's foes will be those of his own household.' (*Matthew 10.35-36*) Again, we are offered by Mark a glimpse of Jesus' attitude towards his own family: 'And his mother and his brothers came; and standing outside they sent to him and called him. And a crowd was sitting about him; and they said to him, "Your father and your brothers are outside, asking for you". And he replied, "Who are my mother and my brothers?" and looking around on those who sat about him, he said, "Here are my mother and my brothers! Whoever does the will of God is my brother, sister, and mother." (*Mark 3.31-35*)

Discipleship requires a radical freedom, and the real 'family' of Jesus are those who follow the gospel's demands – which include the freedom to mix, as Jesus did, with the poor, the oppressed, the rejected. The gospels are clear that the kingdom belongs to them; and those who 'sat about with' Jesus were more likely to be tax-collectors, sinners, and various 'bad characters'(see *Mark 2.15-16*).

The contrast between the church's concern with authority and power and Jesus' subversion of it, is central to Graham Shaw's provocative book *The Cost of Authority.* Shaw remarks that 'whilst Paul verges on hysteria in his sexual prohibitions, Mark represents Jesus as being the object of intense female loyalty and devotion'.[14] So it is not surprising that we find in the teaching of Jesus a very different view of marriage from that in the Pauline tradition. Even the far more conservative commentator, Kenneth Kirk, could comment on the grudging tone of Paul's writings on social institutions such as marriage: 'There is little sense of the dignity of Christian wedlock, or its potentialities for bringing new virtues to light.'[15] Graham Shaw quotes *Mark 10.6-8* and then comments, 'Jesus' teaching has an almost brutal simplicity: physical sexual intimacy, sealed by the existence of children – the "one flesh" of which he speaks – creates a relationship with irreversible implications and obligations. Contrary to the impertinence of the marriage service, the solemn words "what God has joined together, man must not separate" (*Mark 10.9*), do not envisage the intervention of a priestly hand, and this raises the most radical questions about the propriety of using church authority to bless and sanctify marriage of any kind.'[16] This, Shaw suggests, is in marked contrast with the stance of the Church, where 'conformity to a pattern of sexual behaviour has given the church its social visibility and identity. In blessing, regulating and policing that conformity, the clergy have exercised control at the most intimate level of human experience; and they themselves have derived much of their prestige by exemplifying the conformity they demand. By a cruel irony Christianity has thus created its own parody of that Jewish religious authority with which Jesus struggled.'[17] So once again we see that what the Church does has little to do with the gospel and much to do with social respectability and the preservation of its social visibility at a time when that is under threat. As Graham Shaw remarks, 'while the church likes to speak of blessing, it is also conferring respectability, and it is difficult to distinguish the content of that blessing from its attendant social expression and advantages.'[18]

An American church report on homosexuality held that 'human life is held in coherence, saved from collapse and chaos by the order of marriage, family, and society – which are structures maintained by our belief and divine grace ... The orders of life are configurations requiring energetic commitment to sustain.'[19] Here a kind of natural law argument is used to give divine sanction to the status quo instead of recognising, as Shaw does, the radical inversions of the Kingdom. Such arguments can lead to remarkably complacent views of human institutions, such as slavery, racism or the place of women, which the church ought rather to critique and challenge. And indeed today there is growing evidence of 'collapse and chaos' within the family itself. In a 1988 article in *The Guardian* newspaper[20] Melanie Phillips commented that 'the notion that a structure of father, mother and children is by definition a civilising force that always tames base and primitive instincts takes a bit of a

knock from cases such as those in Chester Crown Court reported
this week in which two fathers raped and buggered their children,
in one case with the active collusion of the mother. Families
obviously can and do nurture and prosper their members; but they
can also be grievously damaged and inflict further damage upon
themselves.' 'Parenting,' Ms Phillips observed, 'is hard in a moral
vacuum.' Sure: but 'the family' is not itself a God-given moral or
social glue; it is rather an historical social institution standing in
need of honest critique, a critique which would recognise openly
and honestly that cruelty in marriage and the nuclear family is not
an aberrant phenomenon restricted to beleaguered northern council
estates, and that such cruelty requires not simple denunciation –
which is easy – but love and care for those, usually women and
children, who are its victims; and careful analysis of the causes and
forces which help to produce it. Significantly, Melanie Phillips'
piece (written in the wake of the Butler-Sloss enquiry into the
Cleveland affair) remarks that a paediatrician, Professor David
Hull, 'berated the three clerics who gave evidence to the enquiry
and who remarkably failed to condemn sexual abuse of children
as a sin, evil, or just plain wrong.' It may be, of course, that these
'clerics' were concerned primarily with the interests of those
unfortunate couples who had been wrongly accused of sexually
abusing their children and who had turned to the church for help;
or that Professor Hull was playing a look-for-someone-to-blame
game in which the church is as always an easy target. The truth is
never easy, rarely comforting or comfortable, and never reducible
to some easy formula or slogan. The churches should be involved
in the struggle, sitting alongside those who are its victims, neither
colluding in simplicities nor ducking moral issues, especially
where cruelty is involved. Jesus, we recall, sat with the lonely,
the confused, the rejected, all those who were the victims of a
religious and social establishment which, in Graham Shaw's
analysis, protected its own power and prestige by creating taboos
of rejection and fear: 'the prestige of the religious is purchased at
the cost of the stigma of those against whom they discriminate,
and with whom Jesus identifies himself in the most public and
effective manner.'[21]

Again, much publicity has been given to those 'Christians' who
have characterised AIDS as God's punishment on those who flaunt
'natural' sexual and familial patterns. In a *New Society* article,[22]
David Clark pointed out how gay men with AIDS have had great
difficulty in finding carers at a time when the hospice movement

attracts great public support) because of social attitudes towards them and their illness. Clark comments:

> In some cases, the families of gay men with AIDS have refused to give help of any kind; in others there have been last-minute reconciliations, precipitated only by the imminence of death. For some, to come out as having AIDS will be the first acknowledgement to parents and other family members of being gay. Disfigurement and early death, coupled with stigma and ostracism, may draw some families together; it is equally likely to push others apart. This psychological toll on lovers, spouses, friends and kin is still largely anacknowledged and is ignored in particularly offensive ways by those who talk of the relatively small numbers who have died from AIDS.

This tragic story, made up of countless individual tragedies, is one example of the kind of pressures which are created by contemporary politico-religious dogmas about 'the family'. And these will remain 'largely unacknowledged' so long as we retain a political and theological commitment to 'the family' as being, in Mrs Thatcher's famous words, 'a little piece of heaven here on earth'.

I am not concerned here to deny or to detract from the fact that for many marriage and the family can and should still be a secure and fulfilling arena for personal relationships and social growth, companionship and the balanced and stable upbringing of children: as Kenneth Kirk said, an institution with 'potentialities for bringing new virtues to light'. And we will continue to deplore our high divorce rate, with the attendant distress for those involved, especially children. But such phenomena cannot be properly addressed by a simplistic blanket response, either of hand-wringing denunciation or of well intentioned attempts to liberalise the marriage in church of divorced people. Instead we need to work harder at understanding the causes of these tragedies, and at unmasking the social, political, economic and sometimes religious pressures which result in the individual cruelty. The church will do better in setting out to name these demons, and to be with those who are their victims, showing God's love and care for them as for all who are the victims of human greed, selfishness and stupidity, than in colluding with sentimentalised and guilt-inducing fantasies about the sanctity of family life. A prophetic church, which sits where Jesus was, should hear and give expression to the angers, the frustrations, as well as the hopes and the joys, of contemporary life

in all its confusion, complexity and perplexity, in a way which is
honest, calm, and unencumbered by fantasy.

1 Gareth Stedman Jones, *Languages of Class,* CUP, p.226. The quotation at the
   headof this piece is from the same source.
2 Alasdair MacIntyre, *After Virtue,* Duckworth, p.240.
3 Jones, op. cit., p.220.
4 *ibid.*
5 MacIntyre, *ibid.*
6 Juliet Mitchell, quoted in Lynne Segal, *Is the Future Female?,* Virago Press, p.6.
7 Maud Pember Reeves, *Round about a Pound a Week,* Virago Press edition
   1979, pp. 163-4.
8 c.f. the discussion of the 1987 General Synod debate on sexuality in Peter
   Selby, *Belonging,* SPCK, ch.6.
9 Susan Brooks Thistlethwaite, 'Every Two Minutes', in Letty M. Russell ed.),
   Feminist Interpretation of the Bible, Westminster 1985.
10 See for example the privately produced report 'Breakdown of Clergy
   Marriages' by Hilary M. Devereux, 1985.
11 Blackwell, 1986.
12 John Gillis, 'Weddings Great and Small', *New Society* 18th July 1986.
13 *ibid.*
14 Graham Shaw, *The Cost of Authority,* SCM Press. p.234.
15 Kenneth Kirk, *The Vision of God,* Longmans, 1928, p.76.
16 Shaw op. cit., p.236.
17 *ibid* p.235.
18 *ibid* p.237.
19 qtd. Don Browning, *Religious Ethics and Pastoral Care,* Fortress Press, p.88.
20 Melanie Phillips, 'Pity the battered family', The Guardian 15th July 1988.
21 Shaw op. cit., p.228.
22 David Clark, 'AIDS and the Family', *New Society* 27th May 1988.

Marriage and love in scripture

Janet Wootton

The Hebrew Scriptures abound with love poetry, which is from time to time erotic, breathtakingly emotional, and deeply tender. Frequently this beautiful and moving poetry is used to describe the relationship between God and the people of God.[1]

Alongside the beauty of the love imagery and poetry is a rigid social and moral code, fixing the relationship between women and men and children, in the community of the people of God, as it developed from patriarchy through the charismatic leadership of the judges to the monarchy. In every kind of community, women and children were defined in relation to men as fathers and husbands. Infidelity with, or on the part of, a married woman was the most serious kind of sexual sin, since it questioned the paternity of children.

Again, the image is applied to God's relation to the people of God. Unfaithfulness in religion is likened to the infidelity of the married woman against her husband.[2]

The Celebration of Sexuality

I know a couple - very serious young Christians - who decided that they would read through the whole Bible while they were engaged.

They were engaged for a very long time.

However, they decided to reserve the Song of Songs for their honeymoon, and consequently they did not read it beforehand.

To their surprise, when they came to their honeymoon, they were so taken up with the practical application of that book that they had no time to read it, and, to this day, they still have not read the Song of Songs.

But they are keeping up the practice!

Bible Reading for two

Find the *Song of Songs*. If you can, find two copies, in the same modern translation, one for you, and one for your lover or would-be lover. Some modern translations mark the parts 'lover' and 'beloved', or, 'man' and 'woman'. If you are of the same gender, you will have to decide. There is also a part for 'friends' or 'the poet'. It is probably a better idea not to import someone for the purpose!

Now settle down together, and read this exquisite love song aloud to each other. Some of it will be hilarious - most women today would not thank you for comparing their teeth to a flock of fertile ewes though the image has a certain charm). But here in its fullness is love poetry which is tender, erotic, and very powerful.

Love-language as imagery-Wisdom

Starting from this point, it is possible to look at love-imagery used for God's relation to the people of God as a more realistic comparison. In general God appears as the lover, and the people of God as the beloved - a type-casting which reflects the relative roles of women and men at that time, and which tends to define gender roles in our time.

However, in the Wisdom writings, the Wisdom of God appears as an alluring, charming joyous woman.[3] In an age when women stayed in their own quarters, Wisdom is not afraid to stand on the street corners like a prostitute and call out to the young men as they pass by - not only to call out, but to reach out and try to catch their hands. (*Proverbs 1:20-24, 8:1-4*) She even sets up an alternative brothel with agents working the streets round about.

> Wisdom has built herself a house,
> she has hewn her seven pillars
> she has slaughtered her beasts, drawn her wine,
> she has laid her table.
> She has despatched her maidservants
> and proclaimed from the heights above the city,
> 'Who is simple? Let him come this way.'
> To the fool, she says
> 'Come and eat my bread,
> drink the wine which I have drawn!
> Leave foolishness behind and you will live.
> Go forwards in the ways of perception.
>   (*Proverbs 9:1-6*)

The language of prostitution is deliberately used, partly to counter the destructive trade in women which is seen as the great temptation (*Proverbs 2:16-19,* etc.), but partly also to describe in bold terms the nature and tactics of Wisdom. The image painted is of an independent, powerful woman, well aware of her attractiveness and of what she has to offer, not only to 'young men', but to all people, and even to God, who delights in her. When rejected, she responds with a lover's scorn:

> Since I have called, and you have refused me,
> since I have beckoned and no-one has taken notice,
> since you have ignored all my advice
> and rejected all my warnings,
> I, for my part, shall laugh at your distress,
> I shall jeer when terror befalls you,
> when terror befalls you like a storm,
> when your distress arrives like a whirlwind,
> when ordeal and anguish bear down on you.
> Then they will call me, but I shall not answer,
> they will look eagerly for me and will not find me.
> (*Proverbs 1:24-28*)

Throughout *Proverbs chapter 8*, the identity and power of Wisdom become more and more apparent. Her gifts and fruits are more desirable than anything else - even great wealth. But she has much within her power: she can offer prosperity and political control, gifts which are traditionally in the hand of God.

The secret is told in *verses 22-31*, in another passage of ineffable beauty.

> Yahweh created me, first-fruits of his fashioning,
> before the oldest of his works.
> From everlasting, I was firmly set,
> from the beginning, before the earth came into being.
> The deep was not, when I was born,
> nor were the springs with their abounding waters.
> Before the mountains were settled,
> before the hills, I came to birth;
> before he had made the earth, the countryside,
> and the first elements of the world.
> When he fixed the heavens firm, I was there,
> when he drew a circle on the surface of the deep,
> when he thickened the clouds above,
> when the sources of the deep began to swell,

when he assigned the sea its boundaries
- and the waters will not encroach on the shore -
when he traced the foundations of the earth,
I was beside the master-craftsman,
delighting him day after day
ever at play in his presence,
at play everywhere in his earth,
delighting to be with the children of men.
    (*Proverbs 8:22-31*)

Of course! This woman is the beginning of all creation. Nothing was created except by her.[4] She was the architect of the world and the delight of God and humans.

Love language as imagery - the Prophets

In the prophetic writings, when this imagery is used, God is invariably the male lover, and the people the female beloved. At its theological centre is an extremely sophisticated view of the reciprocal relation between God and his people, expressed in the covenant formula, 'You shall be my people and I shall be your God'. At the time of this development in imagery, that covenant relationship is in danger of being irrevocably broken. So God, the lover, is in the humiliating position of pleading with the beloved to come back to him.

It is significant that the two prophets who became most personally involved in their prophecy (Hosea and Jeremiah) both made full use of this imagery. Hosea even lived it out in his own marriage to an unfaithful woman, discovering for himself the frustration of seeing the one whom he loved, and desired to make happy, forsaking his kindness, and living miserably as the slave of another. He found in his own reaction of alternating pleading and anger, a way of speaking to the people out of God's experience.

Hosea 2 contains both sides of this anguish. It begins in a kind of bitter brutality, which lashes out in anger against the unfaithful beloved.

To court! Take your mother to court!
For she is no longer my wife
nor am I her husband.
She must either leave her whoring ways from her face

> and her adulteries from between her breasts,
> or I shall strip her and expose her
> naked as the day she was born ...
> > (*Hosea 2:4-5*)

This language, violent with sexual jealousy, goes on for thirteen verses, but in the fourteenth, the pain of love answers back as the lover remembers those sweet early days - the honeymoon in the wilderness, when all these other lovers were far away, and Israel and God were alone together.[5]

> But look, I am going to seduce her
> and lead her into the desert
> and speak to her heart.
> There I shall give her back her vineyards,
> and make the Vale of Achor (misfortune) a gateway of hope.
> There she will respond to me as when she was young,
> as on the day when she came up from Egypt.
>
> When that day comes, declares Yahweh,
> you will call me 'My husband',
> no more will you call me 'My Baal' (master).
> I shall banish the memories of the Baals from her lips
> and their name will be mentioned no more.
> > (*Hosea 2:16-19*)

The old marriage bond, the old covenant relationship, will be restored:

> I shall tell Lo-Ammi not-my-people), 'You are my people.' and
> he will say, 'You are my God'.
> > (*Hosea 2:25*)

It is quite an extraordinary insight on the part of the prophet to find such a conflict of emotions in the heart of God.

Perhaps even more striking is the passionate description of the birth and adolescence of Israel in *Ezekiel 16:1-14*. Here, God is the saviour, who finds Israel as an abandoned child, the guardian, who provides for her life.

At birth, the very day you were born, there was no-one to cut
your navel string, or wash you with water to clean you, or rub
you with salt, or wrap you in swaddling clothes. No-one
looked at you with pity enough to do any of these things out
of sympathy for you. You were exposed in the open fields in
your own dirt on the day you were born. I saw you kicking on
the ground in your blood as I was passing, and I said to you as
you lay in your blood: Live! and I made you grow like the
grass of the fields.

When she becomes sexually mature, he falls in love with her and
marries her.

You developed, you grew, you reached marriageable age.
Your breasts became firm and your hair grew richly, but you
were stark naked. Your time had come, the time for love. I
spread my cloak over you and covered your nakedness; I gave
you my oath, I made a covenant with you - declares the Lord
Yahweh - and you became mine.
(Ezekiel 16:4-8)

As in the Hosea passage, the language is not restrained. It is full
blooded and powerful. The full range of sexual and romantic
emotion is expressed, from the tenderness and desire of the
honeymoon period to the pain and anguish of betrayal and separation.

Very well, whore, hear the word of Yahweh! The Lord
Yahweh says this: For having squandered your money and let
yourself be seen naked while whoring with your lovers and all
the foul idols of your loathsome practices and for giving them
your children's blood - for all this, I shall assemble all the
lovers to whom you have given pleasure, all the ones you
liked and also all the ones you disliked; yes I shall assemble
them round you and strip you naked from head to foot ...
(Ezekiel 16:36-37)

Jeremiah stands in the same tradition as Hosea (the Deuteronomistic
tradition), and shares both the personal involvement in his
prophecy, and the image of a marriage between God and his
people. He too describes the period in the wilderness as a time of
courtship and closeness:

The LORD told me to proclaim the message to everyone
in Jerusalem.
'I remember how faithful you were when you were young,
how you loved me when we were first married;
you followed me through the desert,
through a land that had not been sown.
Israel, you belonged to me alone;
you were my sacred possession.
(Jeremiah 2:1-3a)

But Israel has departed from that first closeness, and chased after
other lovers, prostituting herself on the hill tops and along the road
side, the places where local gods were worshipped. Jeremiah's
language is less violent and more sorrowful than that of Hosea.
He shares God's anguish at his people's actions:

And once despoiled, what are you going to do?
You may dress yourself in scarlet,
put on ornaments of gold,
enlarge your eyes with paint
but you make yourself pretty in vain.
Your former lovers disdain you,
your life is what they are seeking.
(Jeremiah 4:30)

In the lovely middle chapters of Isaiah, the language of marriage
and love takes its place among all the imagery of hope. The time
of unfaithfulness, the time of punishment is over, and God takes his
people back. There was no real divorce *(Isaiah 51:1)*, for if there
had been, no return would have been possible. On the contrary,
reconciliation is possible, and the full blessing of marriage and
family life can now begin.

Shout for joy, barren one who has borne no children!
Break into cries and shouts of joy, you who were never in labour!
For the children of the forsaken one are more in number
than the children of the wedded wife ...

Do not fear, you will not be put to shame again,
do not worry, you will not be disgrace again;
for you will forget the shame of your youth
and no longer remember the dishonour of your widowhood.
For your Creator is your husband ...

Yes, Yahweh has called you back
like a forsaken, grief-stricken wife,
like the repudiated wife of his youth,
says your God.
I did forsake you for a brief moment,
but in great compassion I shall take you back.
      (*Isaiah 54:1-7*)

Marriage in the Torah

What is noteworthy in the prophetic literature, besides the passion
of the imagery, is the complete inequality of husband and wife.
The experience of marriage is entirely different for women and
men. The men are the members of the community, the People of
Israel, through a sign, circumcision of the foreskin, which is not
applicable to women. Therefore women belong to the sacral
community only through their relationship to men.

Singleness is not contemplated, except in the case of prostitutes.
Female prostitutes are the only women to have control over their
own sexuality.[6]

The only other unmarried people of marriageable age are those
who have been divorced, or widowed. Divorced women are
eligible for remarriage in limited cases.[7] Widows are the special
care of the community, since they are entirely vulnerable. If they
are childless, and therefore no heir has been born to the dead
husband, the law of levirate marriage requires that the husband's
next of kin marry the widow, and produce sons who are regarded
as those of the dead man.[8]

Marriage is polygamous, but never polyandrous, and a large
number of wives is often a sign of power or wealth.[9] A husband
may also take female slaves as concubines, or, at least during the
period of patriarchy, take the female servant of his barren wife,
whose children are considered to be those of the wife.[10]

The overall aim of the legislation is to control the parentage of
children: to ensure that paternity is known, and so the line of
inheritance is clear; and to enable the begetting of heirs even in the
unfavourable circumstances of infertility or bereavement. In other
words, the legislation is designed to benefit the male community,
to whom it is vital that sons and heirs are continually produced.

Therefore any action which endangers the production of heirs is considered a crime not against the woman who is affected, but against the man to whom she belongs at the time of the wrong. The clearest statement of this is in *Deuteronomy 22:13ff.* Women are divided into three categories: young women still in their fathers' houses; betrothed women; and wives. The first two categories are supposed to be virgins. Young women belong to their fathers, betrothal is the time of handing over to the husband who will be her owner throughout their marriage. The transaction is a financial one, the husband paying a bride price to the father.

A woman who is not proved to be a virgin at the time of marriage is entirely at her husband's mercy. If he demands the proof, and takes action when it is not forthcoming, she is to be stoned to death outside her father's house. The proof is held by the young woman's parents, and, if the husband is found to have accused her wrongly, it is the parents' responsibility to produce it. The punishment on the husband for his false accusation is threefold: a beating, a fine and the loss of his right ever to divorce the woman.

If a man rapes a young woman, again, he is taken to have committed an offence against the young woman's father. He is to pay the bride price to her father, and marry her, again with no right of divorce.[11]

Adultery is a sexual act committed by any man with a married woman. It is the marital status of the woman, not the man, which is definitive. Therefore a married man may resort to a prostitute without committing a capital offence. But if the woman is married, both partners to the act are to be stoned to death.

Illicit sex with a betrothed woman was an offence against the community in the same way as adultery. Both partners are to be stoned to death, except when the sexual act takes place in an open space, where the woman is to be given the benefit of the doubt, since, even if she had called for help, she would not have been heard. In this case, only the man is to be stoned.

Just as the woman is the passive partner in marriage,[12] so she is the passive partner in divorce. *Deuteronomy 24:1ff* describes the procedure for a man to divorce his wife. There is no procedure, nor is the question raised, for a wife to divorce her husband. The procedure is simple, but it does have to be committed to writing. The displeased husband must write a certificate of divorce which becomes the wife's possession, proving that she is free to marry again.

Marriage in the community of Israel

The Hebrew Scriptures, which largely narrate the story of rulers and leaders, lack accounts of ordinary marriages and families. During the period of the monarchy, marriage among the the ruling class becomes almost entirely political, matching Israel's change in status from a 'people' to a 'nation' like the nations.

In the earlier narratives, however, there are examples of less political marriages and lives. The barren marriage of Abram and Sarai is narrated in simple and moving terms. In no sense could the story be told as if it were only Abram's story. Not only is Sarai's barrenness central,[13] but she participates actively in every stage of the narrative. Her connivance is required to keep the whole family safe in Egypt (*Genesis 12:10ff*), and her name is changed as well as Abram's in the second account of the covenant (*Genesis 17:15*).

The account of God's visit, in the person of three men, to announce Isaac's imminent birth, includes some charming domestic detail. Their arrival throws Abraham into a flurry of hospitable activity, in which he runs first to his wife with instructions to begin preparations for a meal. Sarah, though confined to the inner tent, overhears the conversation, and laughs to herself at the very thought of bearing a child at her advanced age. Her laughter embarrasses Abraham, and the narrative ends with a quarrel between husband and wife:

'Why did you laugh? ...'

'I didn't'

'Oh yes you did'
> (*Genesis 18:13-15*)

Much later, after the birth of Isaac, the death of Sarah is told in very moving terms. Abraham weeps over her, and, for her grave, purchases a cave, the first possession of the people later to be known as Israel, in the promised land.

The Wisdom literature also describes ordinary life, albeit the life of the higher classes of society, in homely terms. By and large, the wife is caricatured: Job's nagging wife (*Job 2:9-10*) is reflected in *Proverbs 19:13,* where such a one is likened to a constant dripping.

On the other hand, a good wife is considered a gift from God, and is infinitely preferable to the allures of prostitutes and adulteresses. The dripping tap turns into a store of pure water: 'Drink the water from your own storage-well, fresh water from your own spring.' (*Proverbs 5:15*)

This good wife is described in some detail in the last chapter of the book. Like the whole book, the description is given from the point of view of the husband, who is to cherish his wife 'more than rubies' (*Proverbs 31:10*). From this chapter, it is clear how much of the practical prosperity of the family rested with the wife. In a pre-industrial society, work within the home is valued, even though it does not bring financial or legal independence.

Her work includes manufacture of furnishing and clothing, domestic agriculture, including control over financial resources, and the provision of food and comfort for the household, which consists of husband, children and servants.

Teaching on marriage in the early development of the church

There is no room for the grand, leisurely poetry of the Hebrew Scriptures in the urgent witness of the Greek. The pace and purpose of the New Testament is different. There is a sense of urgency in the earliest writings, arising from the belief in an imminent second coming, before the current generation is past, So all that matters is to preach the gospel as widely and as convincingly as possible. This affects the letters, collected as they flew around the earliest churches, more than the gospel narratives.[14]

What of family relations among the new people of God? What place is there for marriage and its pleasures? The answers tend to be prosaic, and tinged with the asceticism of Greek philosophy, which is, happily, absent from the down to earth nature of Hebrew. *I Corinthians 7* is a masterpiece of balance between the urgency of the times and the natural desires of human beings. Paul, himself unmarried, yet sees the need for others to find the satisfaction of sexual and romantic love.

Now for the question about which you wrote. Yes, it is a good thing for a man not to touch a woman; yet to avoid immorality every man should have his own wife and every woman her own husband. The husband must give to his wife what she has a right to expect, and so should the wife to her husband. The wife does not have authority over her own body, but her husband does; and in the same way, the husband does not have authority over his own body, but the wife does. You must not deprive each other, except by mutual consent for a limited time, to leave yourselves free for prayer, and to come together again afterwards; otherwise Satan may take advantage of any lack of control to put you to the test. I am telling you this as a concession, not an order ...

To the unmarried, and to widows, I say: it is good for them to stay as they are, like me. But if they cannot exercise self control, let them marry, since it is better to marry than to be burnt up.
> (*1 Corinthians 7:1-9*)

If someone with strong passions thinks that he is behaving badly towards his fiancee and that things should take their due course, he should follow his desires. There is no sin in it. They should marry.
> (*1 Corinthians 7:36*)

Poor young people! The moral pressure in these verses is tremendous, and there is no sense - as there is in the Scriptures Paul would have known - of the joy of physical love. Marriage and physical union were to be only out of necessity, not the pleasure of God's gift. Thus the proudly virginal Paul. It would be interesting to know what, for example, Priscilla and Aquila were teaching young couples!

Jesus' example and teaching[15]

The gospels, written, or at least compiled rather later, show the love of God, so vividly described in the Hebrew Scriptures, exemplified in the life of Jesus. There is no longer any need for elaborate and exquisite word pictures of God's love, for there is Jesus, the very expression and fulfilment of that love, in his tender, practical care for the sick and the oppressed, and his outspoken anger against the oppressor.

His own lifestyle was entirely outside the expected norm of the day. Doubts about his own paternity may have been known, since he was called, 'Son of Mary', rather than being known by his father's name. He practised and encouraged an almost brutal disregard of family ties. His response to his mother and brothers, recorded in *Mark 3:31-35, Matthew 12:46-50, Luke 8:19-21,* when they sought him out among the crowds appears heartless to readers today, but is consistent with his response to Peter after the failure of the rich young man to accept his teaching, 'No-one who has left house, brothers, sisters, mother, father, children or land for my sake and for the sake of the gospel will not receive a hundred times as much in this present time . . . and in the world to come, eternal life.' *(Mark 10:29-30).*

At his call, the twelve left everything and followed Jesus. Beyond them, he attracted a wide following of men and women, some of whom, like Martha, Mary and Lazarus, maintained home and family life but welcomed Jesus, while others followed him on his wide ranging journeys.

On the other hand, when he entered into the current debates about marriage, it was to reinforce the laws of sexual control. In the context of the sermon on the mount, which describes the impact of the new community, Jesus emphasises its continuity with the teaching of the old: 'Do not imagine that I have come to abolish the Law or the Prophets. I have come not to abolish, but to complete them.'*(Matthew 5:17)*

A series of examples follow, in which the teaching of the ancestors, 'You have heard it said . . .' is interpreted in the light of the new community, 'But I tell you . . .'.

The examples of adultery and divorce show a hardening of attitude, without any change in the male focus of the commandments. The commandment, one of the ten, against adultery is interpreted, 'But I say this to you, if a man looks at a woman lustfully, he has already committed adultery with her in his heart.' *(Matthew 5:27-28).* Similarly with the divorce law: 'But I say this to you, that everyone who divorces his wife, except for the case of an illicit marriage, makes her an adulteress, and anyone who marries a divorced woman commits adultery.'*(Matthew 5:32).*

However, when the matter of divorce arises in debate, Jesus makes an interesting variation. The story is recorded, with slight but significant differences, in *Mark 10:1-12* and *Matthew 19:1-9.* In Matthew's account, the initiative is still with the male. The ideal is that described in the creation accounts,[16] but permission for divorce was given because of people's hardness of heart.[17] The disciples are horrified! In this case, marriage becomes untenable. In reply, Jesus points again to the radical rejection of marriage and family life which seems to have been his own, and that of some of his followers.

It is in Mark's account that a more radical shift is made. Here it is assumed that not only can a man divorce his wife, but a wife her husband. But in either case, the result is adultery, the breaking of God's law.

What happens, then, in the case of adultery? An odd little inter-polation into John's gospel relates an actual case, in which a woman is brought before Jesus, having been taken in adultery. (*John 8:1-12*). The story is related as a test case, and so forms part of the debate with the Pharisees, who have brought the woman, to see whether Jesus will obey the Law, now obsolete in practice, to stone her.

To our eye, the first flaw is evident. Moses required not that the woman should be stoned, but that both partners should be stoned.[18] As it was required that the people bringing the accusation should have been witnesses to the act,[19] there was no question that the adulterer was unknown. Nevertheless, the accusers waited to see whether Jesus would follow his uncompromising teaching on sexual law with the full punishment required by that law.

Instead, Jesus did a very surprising thing. He changed the location of the sin. The Pharisees had located it in the woman. A male community had found a sinful woman to condemn, and stoning was supposed to eradicate the sinful individual, and with her the sin, from the community of Israel.[20] Jesus suggested that the sin resided in the community itself, and that the stoning of this individual would not remove it. 'Let the one among you who is guiltless be the first to throw a stone at her.' (*John 8:7*).

Even though the woman had been taken in the act of adultery, the charge was dropped, not through insufficient evidence, but because the community was not fit to be her judge. The ideal is still there:

the law still stands, and she is told to 'go and sin no more' - but she goes uncondemned.

In the teachings of Jesus, marriage is part of the ordinary way of life which will be disrupted by the coming of the reign of God, heralded by the revelation of the Son of Man. This disruption is likened to the flood in the time of Noah, at which time, 'People were eating and drinking, marrying wives and husbands, right up to the day Noah went into the ark.' (*Luke17:27, Matthew 24:38*). Inasmuch as Jesus saw his teaching and lifestyle as heralds of the reign of God, marriage and family life had little part to play. However, the laws of the first age still held until the Son of Man should come in all his glory. There is the same sense of standing between two times as there is in the epistles.

Marriage as a sign of consummation

The same sense of a consummation already achieved, but still awaited, finds expression in Jesus' own use of the imagery of marriage.

There is none of the earlier love talk between God and the people. Jesus does not woo people in God's name, as Hosea and Jeremiah did. The nearest he gets is to use some of Wisdom's methods and paraphrase her words:

> Let anyone who is thirsty come to me!
> Let anyone who believes in me come and drink!
> (*John 7:37*)

> Come to me, all you who labour and are overburdened, and I will give you rest. Shoulder my yoke and learn from me, for I am gentle and humble in heart, and you will find rest for your souls. Yes, my yoke is easy and my burden light.
> (*Matthew 11:28*)

Nevertheless, Jesus does talk of himself, as the major prophets talked of God, as the bride-groom. But, unlike the prophetic writings, here the focus is not on his relation to the bride - in fact she never appears in these parables and sayings. Instead, the focal point is the arrival of the wedding day after a long period of waiting. It is the party, and the guests at the party who are important. (*Matthew 9:15, Luke 14:16-24, Matthew 22:1-10*) It is the bridesmaids, whose job is to stay awake and keep their lamps shining during the long wait till the bridegroom arrives.(*Matthew 25:1-13*) It is the best man, who can only rejoice now that the bridegroom is there, and give way to the expected one. (*John 3:29*)

The Bride - missing from the wedding parables - makes her appearance finally in the last book of the Bible as we have it now, almost at the end of the book. The marriage is announced in *Revelation 19:7-9,* with the glad knowledge that the Bride has made herself ready. In *21:10*, after two intervening chapters of judgment, the Bride comes down - she is, of course, the Holy City, Jerusalem, the new symbol of the People of God.[21] There they are, the Bride and the Lamb on their wedding day, awaiting the consummation of all things. The whole Bible ends with the repeated 'Come', sounding like the litany of the end, or the beginning.

> The Spirit and the Bride say, 'Come!
> Let everyone who listens answer, 'Come!' ...
> The one who attests these things says: I am indeed
> coming soon.
> Amen; come, Lord Jesus.
> *(Revelation 22:17a, 20-21)*

The same young couple (remember?) were approaching the year in which they were to get married.

They had been engaged for a very long time.

A rumour started among serious young Christians like themselves that this was to be the year in which Jesus returned, and the world ended.

As fervent Christians, the couple were looking forward to the return of Jesus, which they believed would be soon. But they had waited an awfully long time, and it seemed unfair, somehow.

Secretly, the bride-to-be prayed that the end of the world should not take place till after the wedding!

As you see, it didn't.

---

1   Sadly, the fact that love poetry is used as imagery for the divine/human relation, has been taken as a reason to bleed the eroticism out of the Bible's language of love. The argument should be reversed. The eroticism and romance of the imagery should pump warm blood into the relationship between God and the people of God. This frees the language to mean what it says, and to speak with its full potency. It also forestalls the temptation to 'spiritualize' love poetry which is not part of the image, for example, the *Song of Songs*.

2   Again, the image reflects back on the reality, so that women begin to bear the responsibility for temptation and sin, and become the carries of religious impurity. See, for example, the effect of foreign wives on the kings of Israel: (*1 Kings 11:1ff, 1 Kings 17:31-33 etc.*)

3   The book of *Proverbs* is clearly addressed to young men, and is designed to set them on the path which leads to a kind of moral prosperity. Wisdom appears in female form to counter the temptation offered to young men by immoral or predatory women.

4   The Wisdom of God is one of the concepts behind the complex opening verses of John's gospel.

5   It is an extraordinary insight on the part of the prophet to find this conflict of emotions in the heart of God. The conflict returns in Hosea 11:1ff, this time using different imagery. God appears as a parent the language suggests the mother) of the wayward son, Israel/Ephraim.

6   Two families of words are often translated as 'prostitute'. Qadeshah and qadesh, from the root meaning 'holy', are women and men connected to the Canaanite cult. This practice is condemned as a foreign religious practice as well as on sexual grounds. The word for a woman who earns her living from prostitution is zonah, the male equivalent being celev, meaning a dog. Earnings from prostitution cannot be used for Temple offerings (*Deuteronomy 23:17*).

7   Never to the husband who divorced them (*Deuteronomy 24:4*), nor to a priest (*Leviticus 21:14*)

8   *Deuteronomy 25:5-10.* The most famous example of this is, of course, Ruth from Moab, who returns to Israel with her mother-in-law, and claims levirate marriage with her mother-in-law's kinsman, Boaz. Boaz defers to a nearer relative, who renounces his claim in the time honoured way, by removing his sandal.

9   The fact that Solomon was reputed to have had 700 wives and 300 concubines is related at the end of the catalogue of his wealth (*I Kings 10-11*).

10 There are several instances of this practice: Sarai's maid Hagar Genesis 16) and those of Jacob's wives (*Genesis 30:3ff and 12ff*).

11 There is no sensitivity in the laws relating to young women to the suffering of the woman who is accused or raped. The only question is who has the right and duty to control her sexual activity. Men have the right to expect that each woman will be sexually active with only one man during his lifetime. Therefore the rapist becomes the controlling male, and the raped woman is condemned to a lifetime of marriage to her abuser.

12 A woman is always given in marriage by her father and taken in marriage by her husband.

13 Barrenness was always attributed to the woman, and the accounts always bear this out. So here, it is assumed that it is Sarai who is barren, and Abram fathers a child on the slave girl, Hagar.

14 From the letters emerges a picture of communities filled with excitement, but also faced by the questions of practical Christian living. It is also possible to

trace a development as, perplexingly, the time lengthens, and it becomes clear that the early expectations of the second coming are not immediately to be fulfilled.

15 Jesus' teaching on marriage is not systematic, but arises as he makes his contribution to the prevailing rabbinical discussion of the issues.

16 Jesus uses *Genesis 1:27* from the first and *Genesis 2:24* from the second but earlier) creation account to show that men and women are designed for the close community of marriage.

17 The expression used for their inability to obey God's law - see e.g. *Psalm 95:8*

18 *Deuteronomy 22:22*

19 *Deuteronomy 19:15* stipulates that two or three witnesses must attest to a crime before anyone can be stoned. *Deuteronomy 17:6-7* adds the condition that the witnesses must cast the first stones.

20 Again see *Deuteronomy 22:22* and other instances of laws relating to stoning. This communal form of execution is designed to 'purge the evil from Israel'.

21 Cf Isaiah's use of this imagery to describe the Holy City.

N.B.   Biblical quotations have been taken from the New Jerusalem Bible.

Arise my love and come away

Susan Durber

> The fig tree puts forth its figs, and the vines are in blossom;
> they give forth fragrance. Arise, my love, my fair one, and
> come away ...   *(Song of Songs 2:13)*

A seduction in a garden - the powerful beauty of married love
displayed in the fertile and fragrant garden of the Bible poet. Here
is a fable of the married life and not just of the honeymoon - but of
life's long and languorous journey, when love and limbs entwine to
bring the deepest pleasure and joy. The words of the Song of
Songs, words too little heard in the holy place, speak of a high and
holy and heady experience of marriage, in which desire and duty
meet, bringing forth ripe and luscious fruitfulness. How beautiful,
how beautiful ... Arise my love and come away ...

But marriage is in a mess - or so it seems. In the ugly urban streets
of an inner city parish, where roses grow among the litter, a vicar
conducts no weddings - not since 1986 - though there have been
many babies to baptise. And amongst the princes of our land, the
fairy tale of a wedding all in white ends in bitter tears and a
television mini-series. The fairy godmother has flown and what
was joined has been torn asunder. A registrar tells her tale - of the
groom who says 'see you again next time' - and the twinkle is not
quite bright enough in his eye. And of the gentle teenage brides
who are sold into sorrow and slavery. And those pictures in the
local paper of the couples who celebrate a golden or diamond
anniversary - sixty years was a lifetime when they were born - can
an innocent teenage romance bear fruit yet after so many years?
And the wives who have patriarchs for husbands - lording it in
their private marriage castle - how was it for you dear? And we
must speak not of 'husband' or 'wife' but of 'partner' and find
romance as the film stars do not in marriage, but in adultery.
Marriage is in a mess, an apologetic, sorry, little institution with no
glamour or beauty left - once the dress has been put away and the
cake has turned stale.

But still the Church cries 'marry' - 'better to marry than to burn
with vain desire'. The Christian and political right see marriage as
an institution of safety - a place where children may be raised as

good citizens and where the sexuality of human beings may be bridled and tamed. The Church is still afraid of sex, of the body - afraid of the flesh in which we - let alone Jesus - are incarnated. And so marriage becomes the place where, if the body must be tamed by the will, let it be. Solemn vows are made, decisions of the mind to control the rampant and deceiving body. Better to marry, says the Church, better to marry. And so the Church is in a mess too, fearing the body, hating its messes and it passions, looking for control and tempering desire. The Church's teaching on marriage has, in the past, come from its fear of the erotic. And now in the Church, as in all our culture, we are embarrassed about marriage and silent about its deepest purposes. And in this silence we have lost part of ourselves and lost something deep and beautiful and of God.

Let me tell you about two gardens - two gardens in which a story of love is told. Gardens are good places for lovemaking; the soft grass provides a bed and the flowers give out fragrance to delight us. In a warm and luscious garden, full of the flowing sap and open petals, love stories may be told. The first story is the one we know best, told to us from our mother's knee, told to us as though it were the only story of a man and a woman in a garden. Adam and Eve are in the garden called Eden. At first all is good and lovely and God walks with them in the cool of the garden's evening. But then the garden is filled with shouting and jealousy and God, who is displeased with the man and the woman because of their thirst for knowledge, throws them out. Because the truth of God must be preserved and the will of God must not be thwarted, the woman and the man are barred from the garden of beauty and pleasure. Because of God's jealousy, they must live in the wilderness, where pain and terror dwell, where work is hard and unrewarding and where nakedness is shame. Now the gateway to the garden is barred by an angel with a flaming sword. This is the story which we have been told and the story that shapes our understanding of ourselves. We are those who are ashamed of our bodies, living hard and earnest lives in which eroticism and love must be silent pleasures, lived out only in shame and forgetting.

But here is the second story, another story of a garden in which love is made. This story comes also from the Bible, but it is a story we have hardly heard and which barely made it into the holy book. Here is a garden of unutterable beauty. The garden is filled with fragrant flowers and juice-filled fruits. There are trees and vines, even apple trees and trees for figs. There is spiced wine to drink, honeycomb and milk. Here are henna and saffron - rich colours to charm the eyes - colours to paint the body and perfumes to arouse a lover. Here, in this garden, love is made and tasted and touched. In this garden, as in Eden, there is a tree for lovers to meet under - but it poses no threat and provides gentle shade. In this garden, nakedness is not covered and there is no shame. Here the woman speaks and she longs unashamedly for her lover's touch. There is no expulsion and no taint, and no angel with flaming sword keeps the lovers from their love. The woman and the man are filled with desire for one another and it is good. And God is silent, not jealous of their passion, but caught up within it. 'Arise my love, my fair one and come away ...' Here is a garden I want to walk in, a garden in which a woman can be honest with her desire and where what is beautiful and fleshly and fragrant belongs to us. Here is a garden I want to walk in with my lover. And the Bible gives this garden to me and to you - there is no angel barring our path, no divine decree to keep us out, only the seduction of a lover, wooing us with heady perfumes and lush beauty. Here is a garden I want to walk in.

But the Church has chosen the other garden - or rather it has chosen to lurk at its gates afraid of the angel with the sword and turning to labour and suffering. The garden of beauty and delight is barred for us, not only by the angel, but also by the Church - the Church which makes us afraid of our bodies, afraid of pleasure and delight, afraid to love with passion and strong desire. But I do not want to walk with the Church, I want to walk another way - into the garden of the *Song of Songs*, into the garden of beauty and flesh and desire, into the garden where women and men long for one another with open and godly passion.

But what has this to do with marriage? Everything, I want to say. Everything. For much Christian tradition, we are understood to be souls in bodies; bodies that are tainted by lust and passion, bodies that can be controlled by minds which are trained by God and the Church. We are beasts, redeemed only by the purity of our souls. And so marriage is seen as a holy work of the soul, an act of the will, by which we decide to control our bodies and keep ourselves pure - only unto him. Marriage is the triumph of the will over the body, a control over the brute beasts within us - named so clearly in the traditional Anglican service - a triumph of truth over beauty. In marriage, Adam and Eve are barred from the wild and untamed garden again and held in the sober and barren wilderness of work

and responsibility. Marriage is settling down, a decision, a control
of desire. This is how the church has come to understand marriage,
as an exile from Eden. And this understanding is very strong. The
sensible among us will say 'Do not marry your first love, but marry
your best friend' - the one who thinks as you do. 'Let us not to the
marriage of true minds admit impediment' - true minds. Do not
enter into it thoughtlessly. Make your marriage with your mind
and not with your body. The body is unreliable and tainted by
desire. Marry not your lover, but your friend - then your marriage
will work. And all this has its roots in the garden of Eden.

But there is another way to understand marriage, which has its
roots in that other garden. This is a way which does not fear the
body, its beauty and its passion - but wants to celebrate the life of
the body and to give praise to God through its pleasures and
delights. I want to understand marriage as a place not of safety,
but of danger - as a place not of the will, but of the body, not of
control, but of desire. I want to walk in the other garden, the
garden of lovers. I want to say 'Do not marry your friend - but
marry your lover'. I want to say, 'Your marriage will live in
splendour and fruitfulness not by sharing hobbies, but by sharing
your bodies in an eroticism that is deep and delightful'. I want to
say 'Arise my love, my fair one - and come away - come and lie
beneath the apple tree and breathe in the fragrant air of love.' You
may think that I am romantic and foolish, carried away by the
heady poetry of a little read Bible book and that I should stand
once more before the angel with the flaming sword and understand
where I belong - in the harsh realities of the wilderness. But I
believe that I am right to stand up to the angel and to fight for a
return to Eden, to a return to beauty and desire. For in the Bible
there is this other garden and there are many signs that the
pleasures of our bodies are good and of God and signs of God's
presence with us. We are embodied creatures, fleshly and warm -
and this is how God made us. We are beautiful and we are made
to desire one another. I believe then that we should celebrate
marriage as a covenant between lovers who will worship one
another with their bodies for all their days. It is a marriage not just
of minds, but of bodies: not just for today, but for always, for it
takes time to explore the delights of the garden. And true beauty
and desire come not just for the young and the healthy, the slender
and golden ones. True love is to know the pleasure of the body of
your husband of fifty years and to walk in the garden with the one

who has shared your life's long journey. True beauty is there still in the wrinkling and the grey, true beauty still under the apple tree.

Of course, I am being provocative. But I am being so because I want to change something. Marriage is in a mess and for many reasons. It must be partly that we are frail human beings and that love is fragile and delicate - the solidity of human passion can turn to dust so easily. But I think it is also that we have lost our way to the garden. We engage in frenzies of sexual indulgence, with many partners, as though desperate for something we know we will never find. And marriage looks to many like the boring, middle class, middle brow option - for the sensible, the grey and the controlled. But could it be that marriage might be the place - a life long covenant of lovers - in which true passion is found, the life of the garden not the wilderness? Can it be that in marriage we may find the true pleasure of our bodies, not their taming, but their fulfilment? I believe it to be so. And for those who are not married, and for those who will never marry, perhaps this delight and knowledge of the body will be found in another way - for what human being could truly live without it - enfleshed, embodied creatures of God that we are?

And what of Jesus? Jesus who loved a wedding couple enough to ensure the pleasure of their marriage feast, by supplying the wine in overflowing measure and quality. Jesus spoke of bride and groom leaving father and mother behind and cleaving one to the other. He understood the need to walk in the garden alone. He was one who enjoyed the life of the senses, though as far as we know he was never married, choosing instead another passion. He was also, much more than any of this, the word of God made flesh - God come to share our bodiliness, our desires, our beauty. For such a God, we are bodies as well as minds and it is our destiny to love those for whom our bodies long. For a God of such matchless beauty as ours, we are beautiful children of flesh made for the garden of delight and desire. And in the sacramental sharing of our bodies, one with another, we may sense the ecstasy of the presence of God.

A book which I have read many times is *Testament of Youth*, by Vera Brittain. Vera was young during the first world war and her fiancé, whom she loved with a passion she could hardly name, was killed. After his death, she found in his belongings this beautiful and tender poem. [1]

The sunshine on the long white road
that ribboned down the hill,
The velvet clematis that clung
around your windowsill,
Are waiting for you still.

Again the shadowed pool shall break
In dimples round your feet,
And when the thrush sings in your wood,
Unknowing you may meet
Another stranger, Sweet.

And if he is not quite so old
As the boy you used to know,
And less proud, too and worthier,
You may not let him go -
(And daisies are truer than passion flowers)
It will be better so.

I no longer believe that daisies are truer than passion flowers.
The Church has tried to make marriage the daisy and to bar our
way from the passion flowers. But I want us to storm our way
back into the garden, to cast aside the angel with his flaming sword
and to lie under the apple tree. While passion flowers adorn our
heads, we will make chains with the daisies, and taste the delights
of love. It is in the garden that marriage belongs, as the true and
beautiful gift of God for us - God's fleshly and soulful children. In
the bringing together of fidelity and passion, the garden will bring
forth its fruits. 'Arise my love, my fair one, and come away.'

---

1   R. Leighton in V. Brittain, *Testament of Youth,* Wideview, 1980, p.253.

How is God involved in marriage?

Martin Cressey

How is God involved in marriage? 'In any marriage by creation, by covenant and by divine love: in the marriage of Christians also by grace through faith'- such is the answer about to be spelled out in this chapter. The spelling out is essential, since the brief answer is misleading. It does not mean, for instance, that grace is absent from the marriage of those who are not Christians: 'grace through faith' is to be used as a phrase pointing to the ideas set out in such passages in the New Testament as *Ephesians 5:22-33* and to the discussions centring round the concept of marriage as a sacrament.

Marriage and creation

'... in the beginning, at the creation ,'God made them male and female'. That is why a man leaves his father and mother, and is united to his wife, and the two become one flesh". So Jesus, in *Mark l0:7-8,* takes up the accounts of creation in *Genesis 1 and 2.* He is answering questions about divorce and goes back behind the rabbinic discussions of the Mosaic law to what he declares to be basic, primordial.

This point does not depend upon a particular reading of the Genesis stories. Jesus' teaching is an affirmation of what we human beings are essentially, by God's will. We are by nature relational beings and in particular capable of that relationship which unites a male and a female both sexually and in life partnership; marriages are "made in heaven" in this general sense, that marriage is an expression of the way we are as human beings (this does not settle the question whether particular marriages are a matter of guidance). Of course the very context of Jesus' saying is a reminder that human relationships do not all endure, that marriages reach a point where hardness of heart, "stubbornness", brings breakdown. It is part of a Christian theological account of marriage to assert that such breakdown is a consequence of human sin, rather than a reflection of a natural sexuality which is promiscuous. Yet the theological account is an account of our human physical, psychological and sociological asserts that a particular account of that make-up is true and reflects God's will for us, rather than expressing a moral ideal unrooted in the way we are.

Theologians develop this theme by pointing to aspects of human relationships which can be presented as expressions of what Emil Brunner called 'an order of creation' in marriage. In *The Divine Imperative*,[1] Brunner emphasised the existential link between parents and a child, a 'trinity of being' and the bond between a man and a woman created when human sexual love reaches for fidelity. He saw these two 'facts' as the realities to which the Christian understanding of marriage can draw attention in commending itself. Let us take them in turn, not confining ourselves to Brunner's particular way of treating them, which reads oddly at this distance of time and with all the social changes precipitated by the second World War between us and him.

Biologically the human species, with its relatively long period of gestation and the many years of vulnerable growth to maturity, depends upon a structure of parental and communal care for the young. Even in highly developed communities, where alternatives to parental care exist and can be offered by the state or even claimed by children in a 'divorce' from their natural parents, there is a ready recognition of the depth of the relationship created by a pairing that leads to parenting. The need felt by adopted children to discover their natural parents, the reluctance to break family ties even when abuse or cruelty or neglect have marred them, the loyalties shown in the most trying circumstances can all be seen as evidences of a relatedness built into human life. It is too simple to isolate the nuclear family (Brunner's 'trinity of being'): full human life needs the extended family with all its interlocking patterns and new beginnings ('leaves his father and mother and is united to his wife'). The individuals within the family each have their own significance: the Church has had to learn to value the single person and not to talk only of family. Yet the father, mother, child picture still speaks powerfully in Christian art.

Fidelity in marriage is often presented, in secular as well as religious contexts, as the necessary protection for the child. It has, however, a meaning even before there are children of a marriage and a meaning for marriages which remain childless. This is Brunner's second 'fact', that even in societies where marriages are known to be highly vulnerable, one in three, one in two even, ending in divorce, a couple who are powerfully drawn to one another in sexual love wish for permanency of relationship. It is often those who have experienced divorce who most long for assurance that there is a basis for married fidelity in the purpose of God; hence the pain of rejection by the church or the minister if they are denied a Church wedding. The very existence of that problem for the Church takes us to a second way in which God is involved in marriage, the covenantal aspect of marriage, the marriage vows.

Marriage vows

Christian theology, particularly its Reformed variety, has emphasised God's free commitment to the creation and to humankind within it. God creates by speaking his word and when God speaks, God promises. To those promises human beings respond with their own commitments, to God and to one another. The inter-connectedness of such covenant commitments is well illustrated by the prophecy of *Malachi*. In the second chapter the prophet begins with the responsibility to God of the religious leaders, the Levites: 'My covenant was with him' (Levi): 'I bestowed life and welfare on him, and laid on him the duty of reverence; he revered me and lived in awe of my name' (*v.5*). Now the Levites have turned aside from that course and the whole people is divided in its religious loyalty: 'Why then are we faithless to one another by violating the covenant of our forefathers? Judah is faithless ... in marrying the daughter of a foreign god, Judah has violated the sacred place loved by the LORD' (*vv.10-11*) The use of the marriage analogy for the relation of God with his people leads on to the covenantal account of human marriage itself:' ...the LORD has borne witness against you on behalf of the wife of your youth. You have broken faith with her, though she is your partner, your wife by solemn covenant. Did not the one God make her, both flesh and spirit? And what does the one God require but godly children? Keep watch on your spirit, and let none of you be unfaithful to the wife of your youth' (*vv.14-15*).

Malachi's oracle addresses a particular covenanted nation, Israel, but there is an awareness within it of humankind as a whole ('my name is great among the nations, says the LORD of hosts', *Malachi.1:11*). A covenantal conception of God's relations with humankind throughout history is present in Genesis with the story of the covenant with Noah after the flood, a story which includes the renewed commandment to be fruitful and increase in number and leads into the genealogy of the families of the sons of Noah. It may have been with the Noachic covenant that the writer of Acts connected the rules given to Gentile converts (*Acts 15:20*) and these include a prohibition of fornication. When the Reformers set aside the teaching that Christian marriage is a sacrament (on which see the last section of this chapter), they returned to an emphasis upon marriage as a contract. This had had its place in mediaeval theology also and the contractual should not be seen here as the secular or civil aspect of marriage but rather as its covenantal form, set within a range of covenantal orderings of human life under the overarching providential promises of God.

This approach to marriage enables the Christian minister to affirm God's involvement both by creation and by covenant in all marriages, not only in the marriage of committed Christians. Furthermore, the promises of God spring from a free expression of love for humankind, and it is theologically appropriate to speak at any marriage service of the love of God and of God who is love as well as of the love which has drawn the human couple together to make their covenantal contract.

"Those who live in love live in God"

Both the *URC Service Book* and the *Alternative Service Book* of the Church of England use as an opening sentence for the marriage service I John 4:l6b 'God is love, and those who live in love live in God: and God lives in them'.[2] This is a bold choice for churches whose ministers conduct many marriage services for couples who are not regular worshippers and do not claim to be well-instructed Christians. Many who seek 'a church wedding' frankly say that they are following only a vague sense that there is something more to marriage than a civil contract, something which 'brings God into it': is it right in that context to start from affirmations about the divine love, 'agape', concerning which John wrote, 'If anyone acknowledges that Jesus is God's Son, God dwells in him and he in God. Thus we have come to know and believe in the love which God has for us': these preceding words (*I John 4:15-l6a*) can suggest two different ways of reading the statement that, 'those who live in love live in God'.

On the one hand it can be argued that 'agape' ,being defined by the love shown by God in sending his Son as a sacrifice to atone for our sins (*v.l0*), is only reciprocated by those who have by faith received the divine forgiveness and salvation. It is also possible to read the argument as leading from the knowledge of God's love in Jesus Christ to the affirmation of the universality of that love, the affirmation that, 'All deep human love strikes down somewhere into the Divine, though it may strike darkly and with a dim feeling after Him who is not far from any one.[3] It may be that the latter approach is supported by the fact that after the statement about 'dwelling in love' the writer goes on to claim that 'love has reached its perfection among us' (v.17): John seems to be saying that the love which has reached maturity in the Christian community to which he writes can have many incipient forms in the general life of humankind.

However we take that point of exegesis in *I John*, there is a strong tradition of Christian reflection on human relationships and upon marriage in particular which relates the forms of human love to the divine love and sees God as involved wherever love is. This tradition does not ignore the distinctions which can be drawn between friendship (Greek 'philia'), love for a desirable object (Greek. 'eros') and freely given love, which may reach out to the unworthy (N.T. Greek. 'agape'). The distinctions are not carefully observed even in the language of the New Testament: but more importantly it is possible to observe one kind of love merging with another in human experience and therefore to affirm an outreach of divine 'agape' in and through the variety of human emotions, relationships and commitments which make up the 'love story' of humankind.

Powerful expression is given to this understanding of human love in relation to divine love in Professor John Burnaby's study of the religion of St Augustine, *Amor Dei* .[4] In the Epilogue (p.301ff.) there is an evocation of the stages of human development through childhood to maturity as a discovery of the true relation between love and the good: love 'appears first as reaction to the given good' (parental care),' then as impulse to embody the good idea' (growing creativity), 'and finally as purpose to be served in patient devotion' (p.305): how does marriage fit into such an analysis? Its love is 'a love of conscious preference', not 'an impulse to do good without regard to anything in the nature or character of the person who is to receive it'. Yet, says Burnaby: "If you are really 'in love', you are not pre-occupied with the satisfaction of your own need. You believe that you have found something supremely worthy to receive the best that you can give, something that demands from you a complete devotion ... The love of a man and a woman for one another is a creative act in which through mutual self-giving each is born anew" (p.308-9). Of course, as Burnaby fully agrees, marriage can fall away from its ideal, but "no one altogether incapable or ignorant of philia, of love received as well as given, is in a way to have Agape" (p.310). It is on some such basis as this that the Christian affirms the life-giving presence of God in all marriage, however harshly human self-centredness crowds it out.

Burnaby's account assumes that marriage is the outcome of the personal choice of the partners', 'conscious preference'. It is well to recognise that for many people throughout history and still today, including many Christians, marriage is the outcome of choices by two families, planning as best they can for a daughter and a son. For all the hazards of arranged marriage, there is ample testimony that it can be the setting for a growth into love. God is involved in the families who arrange and with the partners who enter into the arrangement: t he story of the bringing of Rebecca to Isaac (*Genesis 24*) is a love story, though in a mode very different from most of the ones we know in the circles of the URC! And that mention leads to the question - what is different about the marriage of Christians?

By grace through faith

The Christian good news is that God has intervened in human life to save by grace through faith. Salvation is a refashioning of our life, a new birth from above; we are saved from sin, from ignorance, from inability to do God's will, sometimes from pain; we are saved for abundant life, joy, strength, peace with God and one another. The letters of the New Testament almost all follow a pattern of explaining the gospel of salvation, with particular application to some groups of recipients and their situation, and then describing a community life which reflects the changes brought by the gospel. References to marriage come in these latter parts of the letters, along with discussion of the relations between rulers and subjects, masters and servants, parents and children. In one sense everything is changed in these relationships, because they are conducted in a Christian way, 'in Christ'; in another sense nothing has changed - it is still masters and slaves, parents and children, husbands and wives who live the Christian life, though all have equal access to salvation (see *Galatians 3:28*).

The assertion that there is something basically different about a Christian marriage has usually taken the form of the claim that it is a 'sacrament'. This is meant in the strong sense that 'marriage contracted in the faith of Christ has the ability to confer race which helps in the carrying out of those tasks which are demanded in marriage.[5] When Aquinas expressed this view, at the end of the thirteenth century, he still regarded it as debatable, though probable. It was the Council of Trent which in 1563 fixed the teaching, declaring against Luther and Calvin, "If anyone says that matrimony is not truly and properly one of the seven sacraments ... or that it does not confer grace, let him be anathema".

Luther in 1520 had declared, "It is nowhere written that he who takes a wife receives the grace of God. Calvin was more positive, writing in his commentary on *Genesis 2:18* "Moses now explains the design of God in creating the woman; namely, that there should be human beings on the earth who might cultivate mutual society between themselves".[6] This rather arid debate set off from the use of the Latin word "sacramentum" to translate the Greek "mysterion" in *Ephesians 5:32*. The writer has described Christian marriage by comparing the relationship of husband and wife to that of Christ and the Church; he ends by quoting *Genesis 2* 'the two shall become one'" and adding "this is a great mystery, and I take it to mean Christ and the Church". It has been found helpful ecumenically to seek out the meaning in terms of a relationship transformed by the ministry of Jesus Christ. Thus the WCC report *Church and World*,[7] says, 'the relationships of husband and wife, parent and child, master and slave, all commonly seen in terms of power of the first over the second, are to be transformed by the self-giving love of Christ. It is in the new manner in which Christ is head, in the new manner in which the church is subject to Christ, and not according to the customary human patterns, that relationships are to develop within the Christian community. All power and relationships are to be transformed on the basis of Christ's love for the church and the church's love for its Lord'.

This view suggests that there is a continuity between marriage as an order of creation and Christian marriage under grace consciously accepted by faith, just as there is a continuity between human life before and after acceptance of salvation by grace through faith. Paul speaks of himself in terms of "I, yet not I but the grace of God that was with me" (*I Corinthians 15:10*, AV). Christian marriage partners can say "We, yet not we but the grace of God that was with us". Without deciding whether the marriage rite "confers grace", Christians can join in affirming that God in Christ is gracious in all aspects of life, including Christian marriage.

Within such an agreement, there will be as many variations as there are differences in understanding God's providence or guidance. Some believe that God providentially chooses or calls marriage partners for one another: others see the choice of a marriage partner as one of the freedoms under principle that are given 'in Christ' to be prayerfully, joyfully and wisely used! Accordingly we may say either "They were meant for each other" or "It's great that they got together".

The same link with the doctrine of providence can throw light on the question of indissolubility: 'what God has joined together, man must not separate' (*Mark.10:9*), but what is the nature of that joining? Those who name marriage a sacrament generally conclude that the rite and its consummation confer grace in such a way that what has been done cannot be undone, however the human partners or the law may seek to change things. In the language of providential grace, it may be said rather that God has provided strength for the marriage to continue and prosper but that grace is offered, not imposed, so that what none should separate and none outside the partnership can separate (it is both "not-to-be-dissolved" morally and "indissoluble" providentially) can, sadly, be let go or destroyed from within.

So God is involved in marriage in many ways. No marriage is outside God's loving care; no marriage is without traces of the divine love at work in God's creation. Every Christian marriage is under grace consciously accepted by faith and celebrated in the marriage service, indeed whenever the marriage partners worship together. Every marriage is also a vulnerable enterprise of human beings given freedom to receive or to reject the love of others and the love of God. It is with this fragility of human relationships that God has chosen to weave the web of providence.

"Like angels in heaven"

Marriage is temporal, not eternal. The trick question about the future state of a woman and the seven brothers to whom she was successively married left Jesus untroubled. "You know neither the scriptures nor the power of God. When they rise from the dead, men and women do not marry; they are like angels in heaven" (*Mark 12:24-25*). To personally serious questions about whether beyond death we shall recognise and share life with our marriage partners or our parents or our children or our friends, there seem to be no sure answers. Perhaps the best we can say is that the relationships we know on earth give us glimpses of a divine love and grace that will not deal less well with human beings in the future than in the present, so that it will not be a mockery to be "invited to the wedding banquet of the Lamb" (*Revelation 19:9*).

1. Emil Brunner, *The Divine Imperative,* E.T.London, 1937, chs.xxxi and xxxii
2. The URC *Service Book* and the *Alternative Service Book* of The Church of England, ASB.
3. G.G. Findley, *Fellowship in the Life Eternal: an Exposition of the Epistles of St John,* London, 1909, p.370.
4. Professor John Burnaby, *Amor Dei,* London, 1938.
5. Aquinas, *Supplementum,* q.42, a3.
6. J. Dominian, *Christian Marriage,* London, 1967, pp.32-3, P.83.
7. WCC report *Church and World,* Geneva, 1990, ch.V, para.40, p.59.

(Scripture references to REB unless otherwise indicated)

A marriage made in heaven?

Frances Young

Pluralism is a fact of modern life, and most people have adopted
the stance that tolerance of other people's views is an essential
virtue for society to survive. That is doubtless true. The trouble is
that it leads only too easily to a wishy washy relativism, and people
cease to think it matters what a person believes. Religion is treated
as if it were a question of choice, like selecting a brand from the
supermarket shelves - it all depends what suits you, and if none of
them do, you don't have to bother with it at all. At that level,
couples can easily permit each other to differ: one goes to church
on Sunday, the other doesn't, and the one who does won't insist
when they are away together on holiday!

But that only works if religious faith is not taken too seriously.
Since Christianity, or indeed Islam or atheism, actually makes truth
claims about the way the world is, such superficial compromise is
not ultimately satisfactory. A profoundly different perspective may
well be brought to bear on all sorts of issues if one partner has the
kind of religious commitment that deeply informs their life and
their identity and the other does not. Response to that situation
requires much more than bland tolerance. The foundation of
marriage can only be found in a profound respect for the 'other', a
preparedness to listen, a readiness not to try and impose one's own
outlook on someone else. Paradoxically, in my experience, that
situation is a sure way to expose the fact that there are fundamental
common values shared by all decent human beings. Many non-
religious people have a greater sense of duty and loyalty, and are
far more generous, socially committed and caring, than many
claiming the name of Christ - 'By their fruits you shall know
them,' and my husband will enter the gates of heaven before I do!

However, despite that reality, such a situation imposes particular
demands and challenges on the believer who cares. Many fellow-
Christians will hold exclusivist views, and may even officiously
enquire about conversion of the unbeliever. That is bound to put
the pressure on, create uncertainty in the believer's mind, and
could be deeply damaging if a response is not clearly thought
through. Other fellow-Christians may compound all that by
quoting texts, such as 'Do not be unequally yoked with

unbelievers'. (*2 Corinthians 6:14*). Even apart from outside pressures, the very respect in which the partner is held poses questions about the truth, and particularly certain aspects of Christian belief. How can you be sure that God is real when the person you love and respect enough to marry, does not share that conviction? Can you really believe in an eternal salvation worth having, if your partner is excluded? If your partner is a better person than you are, what difference does it make being a Christian? The smug answers trotted out in Christian groups cease to satisfy. You cannot avoid becoming a theologian. You need to discover answers, to explore the resources of the faith and the scriptures to see if the Christian tradition provides any understanding and reassurance.

That standard biblical text (*2 Corinthians 6:14*) hovers there as a potential threat. What are we to make of it? I confess I simply ran away from it for years, offering the answer that Paul's world was different from ours, and not everything in his Epistles is still applicable - rather like most people's treatment of women wearing hats in church! Then it so happened that as a Biblical scholar I found myself working on 2 Corinthians, and that text became part of a whole project. What I discovered was that there is nothing in the context to suggest that this refers to marriage, and indeed it makes far better sense of 2 Corinthians as a whole to think Paul was referring to something totally different.[1]

In any case, elsewhere (*1 Corinthians 7.10-16*), Paul discourages converts from breaking off marriages with unbelievers, suggesting that the unbelieving partner may be 'sanctified' or 'saved' by the marriage, and the children consecrated. Notice that Paul does not say 'converted'. That is far too modern and individualistic a reading. 'Salvation' for Paul meant being incorporated into the community (the Body of Christ) which would survive the end of the world and form the nucleus of the kingdom of God, the new creation. 'Sanctification' was being made holy in preparation for that, and that was something God had to do, through Christ. The union of husband, wife and children (all 'of one flesh') meant their belonging together in such a way that if one was incorporated into Christ, the others were necessarily involved, and would catch some of the contagious holiness that was around.

If someone objects that the text is about new converts staying in existing marriages with unbelievers (Paul was dealing with an inevitable situation in the first generation) and that now Christians should marry Christians, I have to say that the general tenor of Paul's teaching is not in the direction of radical separation from the world. In any case he never envisaged our post-Christian situation - he expected the world to be wound up and salvation arrive within a generation! Meanwhile, his sense of corporateness is an interesting challenge to the incurable individualism of modernity, and it helps me to feel that in a way beyond analysis or evidence, I might be an unconscious channel of grace to those who cannot see the world the way I do.

The Bible belongs to a different world. Nevertheless it often triggers important insights. The parable of 'the Sheep and the Goats' is a perennial challenge to Christians who think they have everything tied up. The people the Son of Man acknowledges at the End in the Final Judgement do not know him, nor do they realise what they have done. It is highly likely that the 'poor' they unknowingly helped were understood by the early church to be Christians: for there is evidence that the earliest Judaean followers of Messiah Jesus were known as 'the poor' (the nick- name 'Christianoi' belongs to the world outside Palestine). The idea that value is placed on my husband for his goodness and for his support for my ministry is one that is deeply reassuring. It doesn't matter whether he would see it that way; it does matter that it makes sense within my own Christian perspective.

And that kind of perception inevitably leads to an expanding view of God and of God's mercy. After all, as Christians we do believe, don't we, that God is the God of the universe - the whole universe? How dare we claim that God's interest is exclusively with those of us who happen to articulate a response to the particular Christian call? If we are serious about our truth-claim that God is the Creator, how can we suggest that only certain elected favourites come within the divine providential care? Jesus said, 'Judge not that ye be not judged.' The more assured my own convictions about God, the more I can afford to stop worrying and simply hand over to God in loving trust all those things and people I care for.

But there are two other points worth exploring, because they give the kind of Christian overview which makes sense of family life, as well as life in general, and so enable positive response to the situation on the ground, so to speak. They are points of specifically Christian theology. The first is that unfashionable doctrine of original sin, and the other is the Gospel of grace.

'Original Sin' provides a general perspective of great significance, and one that rings true in experience. We are all 'only human'. Imperfection is part of the way humanity is. We all fall short of the glory of God. Believer or unbeliever, we belong in solidarity with one another as imperfect. No Christian dare claim they are better than another person; 'there but for the grace of God go I'. Such is the basis of a proper humility which can take criticism, accept and offer forgiveness, and no marriage can survive without that kind of realism, least of all when the picture is complicated not only by the feelings of the partners for one another, but by the peculiar emotional chemistry introduced by children.

Let's face it - kids are wonderful, but they are also demanding and infuriating! In them we see the bare-faced self-centredness and uninhibited inconsiderateness that somehow afflicts us all, and which we usually fail to discern in ourselves, justifying ourselves while we criticise or reprove others. Children frighteningly reflect back our selves as in a mirror, and we respond with hurt and anger, desperately trying to make them in the image we would rather have. How important it is that parents should be different, to temper and complement one another! How grateful I have been that my husband and I do not always see things the same way! I have been saved from many a misjudgement, and I can now discern the importance for our adult children of our deep respect for one another's differences - not to mention the indispensable oil of telling humour, discretely poured on troubled waters!

By the Gospel of grace we are alerted to two important insights. The first is that sin is not the end of the story, and time and time again, the scenario of the last paragraph is the context of creative struggle to new levels of mature relationship, between partners, between parents and children, between siblings. The second is that life is gift, that love is offered free, gratis and for nothing, beyond our desert, beyond anything of which we might be worthy, beyond any claim or right, and the only appropriate response is thanksgiving. The best argument for God's existence, as far as I'm concerned, is that there must be someone to say 'Thank you' to. That thought came to me as a revelation in the very early days of my marriage, when I found the challenges difficult and the joys overwhelming. It remains now, after more than twenty-five years of sharing with my husband the challenges and burdens, the sorrows and joys, the problems and graces brought into our family life by having a severely mentally disabled son.

That experience itself highlights our differences. For my husband such a tragedy is simply a chance accident. That the placenta was insufficient and did not communicate enough nourishment and oxygen for normal development was in his eyes no different from, say, a traffic accident causing disablement. Here was a situation that simply had to be accepted and handled in as caring and creative way as possible. For me it was a devastating challenge to the fundamental beliefs which motivated my whole existence: the vision of a God who was both Love and Creator. Without the support of someone so secure and loving as my husband, it would have been hard to come through.[2] Dare I claim that my 'mixed marriage' was made in heaven? From my present perspective it is hard not to understand it as providential. Thanks be to God!

But that's not the way my husband sees it - and that I continue to respect. My deepening faith would not dare to demand that he accept my view of the situation. And I am deeply grateful for his respect for me, and his recognition of the fact that I have to live out my Christian commitment, that it shapes who I am and what I do, that it is part of the make-up of the wife he chose to marry.

---

1. To explain what would take another essay as long as this! But an interested reader could follow it up by obtaining the book that was the result of that project: *Meaning and Truth in 2 Corinthians,* co-authored by David Ford and Frances Young, SPCK, 1987.
2 The story of how I did is told in *Face to Face, a narrative essay in the theology of suffering,* T. & T. Clark, 1990.

Two angels

Graham Cook

In a school classroom in Zambia there was a chart on the wall headed, 'The properties of angles'. Unfortunately, from there on, throughout the chart, the teacher had mis-spelt the word 'angle'. Instead of spelling it 'angle', he or she had spelt it 'angel'.

That afternoon I learned that '90 degrees equals one right angel'; that 'if it is less that 90 degrees it is an acute angel'; (in the course of my ministry I have met many an obtuse angel too); and that 'two right angels make half a revolution'.

That true story provides some convenient hooks on which to hang what I have to say to you both.

Angels

You might not recognise yourselves by that designation. But the word 'angel' simply means a messenger of God. Today that is what you are. In coming to declare yourselves to be husband and wife you are saying something about the purpose of God for yourselves and for other men and women.

Cute angels

One of the reasons you are here is that once upon a time you must have looked at each other and said to yourselves, 'He/She looks kind of cute' (or words to that effect). In other words one of the things you are declaring is that one of the purposes of God is that some men and some women are attractive to each other. That is true for you and it is true for others. You are here to declare that and we are here to celebrate it with you.

That is one of the ways the human race takes a step forward in each generation. Because you are attractive to each other you leave behind father and mother and cling to each other, and create something new.

That will not be easy for either of you. I have known one set of your parents longer than you have, the other set I have met only more recently. But I know them all well enough to understand that they are strong characters and that however long you live there will always be something of them, their outlooks, their values, in you.

But beyond that you two are creating something new, something the world has never seen before; the Alex and Rachel phenomenon. Watch out world!

There will be some here, and certainly some beyond here, who would want to warn you that the passion which has drawn you together will not last forever. For some, that is true. But from my own experience I want to tell you that it can last. Insofar as I am here to give advice, it is this. Of course you are not the only two attractive people in the world. Other men and women are attractive too. They may be attractive to you, and attracted by you. But love is born and continues to be reborn again and again out of fidelity. Faithfulness to each other is the means by which passion flares again.

Obtuse angels

Being married is not enough. Why did we read that strange passage of scripture on your wedding day? Because it says that respectability is never enough. Some people think, 'Because I have never committed murder I am alright'. But that is not enough for Jesus. He always wants to go further and says, 'Do not be angry'. It is not enough to be religious. Some people think that religious exercises are all that matters. But it is not enough for Jesus. 'If, when you are bringing your gift to the altar, you remember that someone has a grievance against you; first go and make peace, and then come and offer your gift'.

Dorothy Sayers once wrote that people can be greedy, selfish, cruel, jealous, unjust, violent, brutal, grasping, unscrupulous, liars, stubborn, arrogant and think that, because they are married all is well. Simply being married is not enough. If you remember that your husband or your wife has anything against you, first make peace, then come and offer your gift at the altar of marriage.

Two right angels make half a revolution

Two people in a world of their own is only half the story.

Marriage is about this new thing which you are creating. It is not only about the new relationship between you as two people. It is also about the relationship which you, as a couple, have with friends, with neighbours, with family, with work, with the world. Because of what is happening here today the world is going to be a different place.

You two are right angels, messengers of God. You are making your lives new, and ours too. That is what we are celebrating with you here today.

This address was given at the wedding of Rachel Burnham and Alex McNeill. The text was *Matthew 5:21-24*.

Reading the Bible on marriage

Susan Durber

There are many books about marriage available in the shops, but
the Bible is not one of them. If we go to the Bible expecting it to
offer us guidelines, advice and instructions about marriage in any
sort of straightforward sense then we are likely to be either
disappointed or misled. We cannot simply read off a theology of
marriage from the pages of the Bible without taking account of its
setting within history, of its very real plurality and even
contradiction and of its wider purposes.

But, it would be just as foolish to pretend that the biblical texts
offer us nothing on the subject or that because of their antiquity
and 'strangeness' they cannot be relevant for us today. The Bible
has been a founding document of our contemporary cultures,
continuing to shape the ways in which we live, sometimes for ill
but also with possibilities for good. The Bible may also continue to
act as a founding document for new ways to live even within our
contemporary worlds. As one of the most important ways in which
we live is within sexual partnerships, we can expect that any book
which shapes the way we live will have something to say, however
slantways, about such partnerships and, in this case, the partnership
we term marriage. There are two positions I want to avoid, both of
which are flawed: the one that says that the Bible has clear
teaching on marriage which we today can simply take for ourselves,
and the other that says that the Bible is an ancient and irrelevant
book containing the mores and customs of peoples so different
from us that we can learn nothing. My stance reflects a desire to
learn with humility from the wisdom of the biblical traditions, but
also to listen for the wingbeats of the Holy Spirit who empowers us
to read the biblical texts with contemporary wisdom.

I also want to engage in the task of listening to the voices of those
whose stories lie on the margins of the biblical texts, those whose
voices are just now beginning to be heard. This means that the
Bible need not be seen as a monolithic text, but as a plural and
shifting collection of sometimes conflicting texts with which we
stand in a dynamic relation. In all this too, I recognise that the
biblical texts, with all texts, do not have such fixed and stable
meanings as a quest for 'what the Bible says about marriage' might

seem to suppose. The reading process is a dynamic one in which the cultures in which we as readers stand meet the marks on the pages of the Bible. We do not read as our predecessors did, we do not read all in the same way, and there is no final, correct and pure reading. So, the project of looking for wisdom about marriage by looking at the biblical texts will be a task marked as much as by creative imagination and struggle as by anything like straightforward research and discovery.

There are, of course, powerful Christians within our cultures who claim that 'the Bible teaches' some very specific things about marriage and that if we live by these all will be well. For such Christians, the way of life may not be easy, but at least it is possible to discern what it is. In a popular book on marriage, *Marriage is for love* by Richard L. Strauss,[1] we read, for example,

> The Bible teaches that marriage and the family are divine institutions, in fact, they were the first institutions established by God... Yours can be a happy Christian home if you will learn and practice the basic biblical principles of marriage. I believe that any normally intelligent husband and wife can enjoy a happy marriage and a successful home life if they learn what the Bible teaches and obey it. Everything necessary to establish such a relationship is found in the scriptures.[2]

Though Strauss recognises that there are differences of opinion about Jesus' attitude to marriage, he claims that the basic intent of biblical teaching is undeniable and he proceeds, as many others have done, to set out in very clear words the way in which he believes Christian marriage should be lived. Such an approach is commonly found but is fraught with problems. If taken seriously, the fundamentalist reading of the Bible on marriage has to face the very real plurality of the biblical texts. It always has to privilege a particular portion of the Bible if it is not to conclude that, for example, polygamy is permissible. So even a fundamentalist reading turns out to include a prior assessment of what constitutes the biblical view. It can never, as it sometimes seems to claim, simply read guidelines from the page. It does not escape the hermeneutical circle. Such an approach is also problematic in that it invariably includes affirmation of the patriarchal traditions within which the biblical texts were constructed. 'The Bible teaches' usually prefaces a reassertion of a 'biblical' notion of 'headship';

the man, of course, being the head of the woman. Such an approach, though it claims simply to represent 'what the Bible says' is just as ideologically constituted as any other and actually functions to uphold the power of the powerful. This approach also fails to take account of the complexity of the task of interpretation. It assumes that ancient texts can speak plainly to us across the years and takes no account of our position as readers in the twentieth century or of the place of the biblical texts as, in some way, founding documents for our cultures. It does not take seriously the hermeneutical questions that have become such a part of contemporary biblical studies and theological debate.

There are also those, of course, who would claim that the biblical texts can have no claim upon us, that they represent the thought forms of earlier and often more barbaric times. It can, with considerable justification, be said that the biblical texts have little to teach us about marriage because they present it from within a thoroughly patriarchal context, in times before contraception was available and in eras when the mutual love between a man and a woman was valued much less than such things as the stability of society and the preservation of national identity. While it is necessary to treat this critique with great seriousness, it is also possible that the variety and plurality of the biblical texts can offer us some surprises. Though teaching about marriage and stories about married people come to us in the biblical texts from contexts very alien from our own, it is just this alienation which may sometimes speak to our contemporary cultures in unexpected ways. Of course, we read the biblical texts and we cannot ignore the dissonance between our context and theirs (or indeed the ways in which the biblical texts have been used to sustain the exploitation of women by men known as patriarchy), but there is also a sense in which these texts may read us. We cannot ignore the ways in which these texts have shaped and continue to shape the cultures in which we stand, just as we cannot ignore the real critiques of some biblical passages which are inescapable today. Our relationship with these biblical books is very complex. We are in no position either to accept the fundamentalist reading or to avoid reading the Bible altogether. Instead, we find ourselves in a conversation with the biblical texts; we read as those who are already read both by the Bible and by our cultures. We can do, in a sense, no other. Such a relationship, I believe, can be a fruitful one.

An important part of the biblical witness is its presentation of the gritty realities of human living. In thinking about what the Bible has to say about marriage, we can first say that the biblical texts present us with very honest accounts of what happens within human relationships. There are biblical passages, notably those recording the words of Jesus, which give us ideals to which we can aspire; of lifelong fidelity and unity, for example. But the Bible cannot be accused of painting an unrealistic picture. The potential and often actual terrors of marriage are graphically portrayed. Within the biblical texts there are powerful and disturbing tales of sexual violence, of infidelity and abuse, of polygamy and prostitution. There are stories such as Abram's abuse of his wife Sarai - giving her to foreign kings in exchange for his own safety (for example, *Genesis 12:10ff*), and of David's lust for Bathsheba, the wife of Uriah (*2 Samuel:11*). There are also within the biblical texts many clear indications of the ways in which the marriage relationship has been a 'place' for the oppression of women (though, of course, it is rarely the author's intention that we should understand the texts in this way). From the book of Genesis, we read of woman being created from man and of having the role of helper (*Genesis 2:15ff*). Even though placed alongside another creation story in which the man and woman are created simultaneously and (both) in the image of God (*Genesis 1:26ff*), this text powerfully proclaims the subordination of women and has been interpreted even within the biblical canon itself as a text which determines the relation of the man to the woman particularly within the context of marriage. There are many passages within the biblical texts which indicate that married women have often been regarded as the property of their husbands. Even the celebrated ten commandments make this assumption; 'you must not covet your neighbour's wife' (*Exodus 20:17*). Within many biblical contexts it is clear that the male partner in the marriage relationship is the one invested with most power and that to be a 'wife' is to be in a position of subordination. Even in the letter to the Ephesians, where the writer is intent on stressing the mutuality of marriage, the domination (or 'headship') of the male partner is not forgotten (*Ephesians 5:22ff*).

This domination of the husband over the wife is also presumed when, as is a common feature of the biblical texts, the marriage relationship is used as an image for the relationship of God with God's people. Though the main purpose of the use of such an image is to demonstrate the intimacy and love which God has with us, hidden within it is the assumption that the wife is in a position of subordination to her husband. It is significant that God is always represented by the male partner and God's partner by the female - the implication is clear. Also, when God's people are unfaithful, they are portrayed by the image of an unfaithful wife (for example, *Hosea 1:2ff*). So, the Bible does not hide from us the realities of marriage as it has been lived within a variety of cultures. The biblical texts do not leave covered the violence and domination that are often a part of married relationships or hide the fact that the source of such things has lain within the themes of the faith itself. They do not pretend that human beings always lead exemplary lives, that they always live according to the same ways or even that the people of God have always understood marriage in the same way. However, it must not be assumed that the biblical texts themselves necessarily present critiques of sexual violence, of polygamy or of patriarchy in ways that we now, as contemporary readers, would devise. Neither must we assume that the biblical texts are 'innocent' - they do not only record what many of us now see as appalling 'texts of terror', but they also, as founding or 'classic' text, contribute towards the construction of cultures in which wives are the property of their husbands, for example. The biblical texts represent well the ambiguous nature of many aspects of marriage and they reveal all too well the ways in which marriage has been lived as an oppressive institution. They are also 'guilty' of perpetuating some of these worst features. As contemporary readers, we should read these texts not only with a wry and knowing smile, but also with a contrite heart.

However, if there is a sense in which we must 'read' the Bible then there is also a sense in which the Bible may 'read' us and even, in a sense, 'read' itself. There are biblical passages which can give us a very real sense of ways in which the marriage relationship can be lived to enhance the life of both partners, of the wider community, and even of God's self. There are some sublime and glowing passages which, though set in the context of tales of terror and oppression, yet speak of ways in which the relationship between a man and a woman lived within the context of commitment and covenant can be a source of life. The account in *Genesis 2* of the creation of the woman, though embedded within a patriarchal understanding of woman as derived from man, also proclaims the possibility of such intimate relations between man and woman that they are as though one being, 'bone from my bones, flesh from my flesh' (*Genesis 2:23*). Here is envisaged much more than the 'good order of society' view of marriage which we often suppose is at the root of understandings from antiquity. This passage can indeed be read as evoking the radical kind of 'oneness' within relationship advocated by the most modern psychiatrist. It effectively points us to the great potential of human relationship which our age, as well as any other, needs to hear. For the editor of *Genesis 2* this oneness of flesh and bone is about more than fleeting sexual union - it applies to the longlasting union of marriage in which a break from parents leads to a union with another. Also for the editor, this union is not 'for the procreation of children', but rather for the good of the relationship itself, for the sake of 'partnership'. Here then, in the stories of creation, we read of the stunning potential of human love when lived in true partnership. The story goes on to tell of the very real struggles at the heart of human sexuality; of its pain and alienation and inequality. But the vision remains and it is a vision worth more than a look. There are also within the biblical texts some good examples of married relationships, even though it has to be said that we rarely hear in any real sense the woman's voice. In the story of Elkanah and his two wives, Hannah and Peninnah, Elkanah does not reproach Hannah for her childlessness (though he cannot be said to be understanding of her sorrow!), but rather he says,

> Am I not more to you than ten sons?
> (*1 Samuel 1:8*)

This could be read as an example of gross insensitivity and arrogance, but it can also be read as an affirmation of the importance of mutual love in the marriage partnership even beyond the very great importance then attached to having children. The writer of *1 Samuel* tells us that 'it was Hannah whom Elkanah loved' (*1 Samuel 1:5*). And who could deny that the *Song of Songs* is an emphatic celebration of the beauty and holiness of the love between a man and a woman? The companions of the bride and groom say,

> We will exult and rejoice in you;
> we will extol your love more than wine;
> rightly do they love you.

> (*Song of Songs 1:4b*)

In *Deuteronomy 24:5* we read that a man who is newly married is to be exempt from military service or public duty so that he can be happy with his wife. Though, of course, nothing is said about the happiness of the wife who has been 'taken', there is a valuing here of intimate relationship which has something very significant to say to us today, even if it comes to us from a flawed context (and what context is not flawed?).

Many passages from the Old Testament as well as from the New declare that the will of God is for permanent and lasting relationships and that divorce marks a very real tragedy of human frailty. There are passages which do permit divorce under certain circumstances, but it seems evident that Jesus, for example, believed that marriage was always a lasting commitment.[3] In their textual and historical context many of the statements against divorce were made in order to protect women from men who wanted to cast them off. For example, we read in *Malachi 2:15-16,*

> ... do not let anyone be faithless to the wife of his youth.
> For I hate divorce, says the Lord ...

This kind of example can hardly be used to deny a miserable woman escape from a cruel marriage. In the New Testament there is a variety of opinion about the possibility of divorce, far broader than the 'hard' sayings of Jesus would suppose. In *1 Corinthians 7:15* Paul advises that a marriage between a Christian and an unbeliever may be ended if the unbelieving partner wishes it. Perhaps it is right to recognise the plurality of views about marriage and divorce within the biblical texts (as well as recognising the significance of the contexts in which such views are held), but also to understand that there are many (for us) 'hard sayings' about the indissolubility of marriage or the sinfulness of divorce which can only be for us, in our context, indicators of the ultimate worth of lifelong commitment within the marriage relationship. The separation or divorce of marriage partners can hardly be said to be 'unnatural', because it happens so often and because fidelity, loyalty and life-enhancing mutual love are high ideals and not easy to attain. But we can at least say that it is good for human beings to live their lives within the context of enduring and deep relationships in which love may be shared within commitment.

We have learnt that it is often right for marriages to end when the relationship has broken down. We know that release from a cruel or dead marriage can be a fruitful thing. But we can also say that there are great life-giving resources to be found in a truly, loving and just life-long partnership. Helen Oppenheimer has written well on the 'hard sayings' of Jesus.

> It is easy to believe that when he was questioned about divorce Jesus talked positively about marriage and took the whole question back behind the law of Moses to the Creation. The centre of the whole matter is that husband and wife shall become one. From this much follows; but what follows is not after all either rigorism or a new and special law for Christians, but the basic unnaturalness of divorce.

> Into this positive understanding of a human tendency, blessed by God, to form 'pairbonds', to vow faithfulness to each other for life and be each other's chosen and fit companions, the hard sayings fit as vivid, characteristic, maybe hyperbolic utterances of the Lord.[4]

While I would dissent from her description of divorce as 'unnatural' and question her apparent desire to be able to agree with Jesus, I affirm Helen Oppenheimer's reading of the 'hard sayings'. We can understand them today, not as rigorous laws, but as strong and even hyperbolic statements which can point us to the real potential value of the marriage relationship. The unity of which Jesus spoke, the becoming 'one flesh' remains a truly life-giving way of life, worth celebrating and encouraging. Though we live in an age which recognises all too well the potential failures of the marriage relationship (the oppression of women it has often entailed, the pain of divorce, the dread of failure), nonetheless we can hear for our age the biblical affirmations of the possible value of marriage; of mutual love, fidelity and partnership lived within the context of real and shared commitment. It also remains significant that the marriage relationship is so often used as an image of the love between God and humankind.[5] Though this image is subject to critique in that it is based on and upholds patriarchal culture, nonetheless it affirms that, for many biblical writers, the marriage relationship was one in which human love could find such a full and intimate expression that it was worthy to portray our relationship with God. We need not share the naiveté and simplicity of Carlo Carretto who could say,

So isn't married love a fine thing; if God chose it to be the human model for the mystical life?[6]

But we can recognise that in sharing the love of a marriage we can come to know something of the love of God. We can learn from many biblical passages that just as the being of God is found in God's love for God's people, so our being may be found in the deepest love that we may ever share. There is much in the Bible which encourages us to understand marriage as a clue to the heart of what it is to be human and even of what it is to be divine.

But, while there are many biblical passages which celebrate the virtues and wonders of marriage as well as those which reveal its perils, there are also significant biblical traditions, particularly in the New Testament, which seem to relativise it - to diminish its importance. This needs to be taken seriously. It seems likely that Jesus himself was unmarried and there are many points in the Gospel accounts where the 'Kingdom' seems to take precedence over everything else, even marriage. In *Matthew 19:12,* for example, we read of those who have 'renounced marriage for the sake of the Kingdom of Heaven'. Jesus talks often of the demands of discipleship and the need to 'leave everything' (though interestingly, in *Mark 10:29* 'wife' is not included in the list of things one might give up) and in *Luke 14:26* we read,

> Whoever comes to me and does not hate father and mother, wife and children, brothers and sisters ...

In the parable which precedes this statement in Luke's Gospel, it is not permissible to be excused from the dinner party (the Kingdom) by saying, 'I have just got married'. In response to a question from the Sadducees (*Luke 20*) Jesus says that marriage is of 'this world'. In the parallel text from Matthew's Gospel, Jesus says,

> For in the resurrection they neither marry nor are given in marriage, but are like angels in heaven.
> (*Matthew 22:30*)

In the writings of Paul too, we can sense some relativising of marriage. When Paul writes in *Galatians 3:28* that there is no such thing as male and female, should we understand this as a denial of the significance of sexual relationships? Paul certainly makes it clear in *1 Corinthians 7* that it is better to refrain from marriage, though it is not wrong to marry. There is a strong sense in this letter that Christians live in the last days and that questions of marriage are put in a new perspective because 'the time we live in will not last long' (*1 Corinthians 7:29*). Paul sees celibacy as a gift from God, but it is not clear whether he sees marriage as an equal gift or whether it is a distraction in the life of the Kingdom.

Though there are many passages in the Bible which affirm the real and lasting value of marriage, there is this significant line, particularly in the New Testament, which questions its final value in the light of the Kingdom. This line of thinking has been important in Christian history as it has been associated with a denial of the 'flesh' and a suspicion of sexuality and, notably, of women. It may be argued that such passages have been interpreted out of context and that they reflect little more than the hyperbolic style of Jesus (a Jesus who also seems to have reaffirm the value of marriage) and the belief of the early church that the Parousia was very near. Nonetheless they have been very influential.

How then may we understand them today? We cannot deny that such a line of thinking has been caught up in a devaluation of the flesh and of women - these are not innocent texts. We may feel that, in different times, we need to affirm other biblical themes which celebrate marriage and sexuality and which do not even imply that celibacy is a higher calling. Perhaps we can also recognise, in an age when the Church in many of its forms seems to value 'marriage and the family' to such an extent that single heterosexuals and homosexuals and lesbians feel excluded from the community, that there are a variety of ways of human living which are faithful to our humanity and to our being before God. It may be that, today, we need, in some places, to hear the 'relativising of marriage' themes from the biblical texts, though for very different reasons from those for which they were first written. In creative ways, the plurality of the biblical witness may echo and affirm the pluralities of our modern cultures.

Many of the questions which theologians have often asked about marriage do not find a ready answer within the biblical texts. Indeed, it often seems that the questions are anachronisms in the plural and ancients worlds of the Bible. Is marriage a gift of God to the Church or is it a 'natural' institution? Is it the man and the woman who marry one another by their promises of faithfulness to

one another or is their marriage effected by God? Is marriage a
sacrament or not? These questions may not be the talk of the
streets today, but neither are they the natural concerns of the
biblical writers. It seems clear that the writer of Ephesians was not
describing marriage as a sacrament or 'mystery', but referring to
the living bond between Christ and the Church (*Ephesians 5:37*).
Though it may be right to conclude that he did regard marriage as
deeply significant because of its power to image the divine/human
relationship, it is wrong to involve him in more 'modern' debates
about whether there are two or seven sacraments. Similarly, it is
true to say that marriage in many Old Testament contexts seems to
have been conducted without 'religious' ceremony, but, of course,
those involved were not modern day secularists. As Schillebeekx
comments,

> 'We could call Israelite betrothal and marriage 'civil' but
> for the fact that, because of her faith in creation, Israel saw
> the hand of God in everything. For this reason it would be
> anachronistic to apply our modern term 'civil marriage' to
> Israel.'[7]

In many biblical contexts, it was quite natural for marriage to be
understood as a natural, human reality, but then also and at the
same time as a gift of God. In many places there is none of the
devaluing of the body and of nature which has often made it
essential within later Christian theology for marriage to be
understood as an act of a good and holy God which redeems fallen
human sensuality. Though Tobit prays for God's blessing on his
marriage before getting into bed, this does not mean that God is
any more involved with marriage than with any other good part of
God's creation. Tobit's asking for God's blessing does not deny
that marriage is fundamentally a covenant between two people who
are engaged in what has been God's purpose for all creation since
the beginning. Tobit does not require an act of God - a blessing -
for the marriage to be made. God's presence is already there in the
covenant relationship, even, one might say, as the witness to this
very human bond.

It would be tempting to conclude, having read the Bible with an
eye to its teaching on marriage, that marriage should be abandoned.
It could be dismissed as an institution of the patriarchs, oppressive
of women, a denial of the freedom and goodness of human

sexuality and an unholy muddle of prudery and prescription. But it may be that reading the Bible with an eye to its finer threads will give us the courage to envision human sexuality and partnership in more life-giving and transforming ways; to see covenanted sexual partners as 'closest neighbours',[8] living out the demands and joys of love and receiving through a 'natural' and secular reality the finest gifts of God's grace. It may be that the Bible texts can become again texts of liberation and sources of wisdom for human living.

1   R.L. Strauss, *Marriage is for Love,* Tyndale House Publishers, 1985.
2   R.L. Strauss, *Marriage is for Love,* p.11.
3   I think we should take the Markan record of Jesus' teaching on marriage (*Mark 10:1-12*) as more 'authentic' than that of Matthew (*Matthew 19:3-9*)
4   H. Oppenheimer, *Marriage,* Mowbray, 1990, p.47.
5   See for example *Ezekiel 16:8* where sexual relations become an image of the covenant between God and the people and *Ephesians 5:32* where the marital image is used of Christ and the Church.
6   C. Carretto, *Made in Heaven,* Darton, Longman and Todd, 1978, p.28.
7   E. Schillebeekx, *Marriage: Secular reality and saving mystery,* Sheed and Ward, 1965.
8   J.P. Bagot, *How to Understand Marriage,* SCM Press, 1987, p.38.

The break up of marriage

Betsy King

When I was divorced, people felt sympathy for me. My husband had gone to a Caribbean island and procured a single signatory divorce without my knowledge or permission. I had clearly been wronged, cast aside and rejected. It was easy to feel sorry for me. In truth, what my husband had done in taking that decision on my behalf was my liberation.

I believed in my marriage promises to the extent that through all the signs of it being the wrong relationship for either my husband or myself, I was going to make it work. I did the compromising, offered the reconciliatory actions, supported us both, raised the children and was grateful for the help when he contributed. We had entered into a covenant which I was determined to honour even if he was not. When he left me, he freed me in a way I had not the courage to free myself.

But for the gifted people who are our children, we should not have married, let alone stayed together as long as we did. We fed on each other's insecurities and lived in each other's pipe dreams. The joy we had in our initial love was the joy at being loved in a way we let ourselves accept. We were both oppressed by the expectations of society as it sees people married off in their mid-twenties, as it sees people acquire the accoutrements of established households, and as it confirms the male/female, leader/follower modes of being. We oppressed ourselves with the expectations of our families, with our own ideas of success and with our individual psychological burdens. We were neither one honest. The Caribbean divorce brought us both the possibility of liberation out of oppression.

Considering the often quoted reasons for divorce, neither one of us committed adultery. Neither one was violent or abusive. Our marriage was consummated. We were not guilty of the seemingly forgivable sins which allow people to become divorced with the blessings of the Church. We fit in no recognised category except the one of those who fell out of love. Even that category is an uneasy fit for us, because I cannot say we were ever honestly in love; in each other we sensed an escape from life up till then and a way of legitimising the physical cravings we felt. We had our own kind of love. The reason for our divorce was that we changed. We just became different people who saw life differently. I began to be desperate for the truth and my husband wanted the dreams he married. We changed. That is all.

So what does the Church do with divorced people? Either one of us can be barred from communion depending on the tradition, neither one of us can be married to another in church according to some traditions and in other traditions we could not even attend church. The Covenant was to be forever according to the liturgy and no matter the circumstances, we have broken a covenant. However, in the marriage promises we made, it was understood that we came to make them in utter freedom. The weight of the covenant should have been known by us as we made the promises. The truth is that we were not free nor did we understand what marriage honestly meant. We only knew we wanted what other people had, what our families expected, what the claims of our bodies needed and what we dreamt would be possible. We made a blind covenant in a church which condoned our action.

In the stories behind the marriages I have conducted in my ministry, I find similar situations. People marry for love or lust, for dreams, for families, for friends and people change. Promises made between people become different promises as people change. It has been said that marriage is a promised relationship where two people change, but hopefully at compatible times. Most of the people who come to my church for marriage come for second marriages where personal changes have not complemented the relationship. Their experience is sometimes of adultery in the first relationship, sometimes painful violence and sometimes injustice in many and varied ways. No matter how faithful partners may have been, it is most often that people changed, learned new truths, grew in different directions and fell out of love. Some fall out of love never having tried. Others try, go to counselling, compromise and yet still cannot live together. Love may still be present, but living together might be impossible. They come in hope that the second commitment will be the lasting one and that they have learned from the first. This will not necessarily be the case; sometimes women and men divorce a reality about themselves that they cannot face. Mostly they come, having experienced change which is incompatible with the original partner, feeling guilty about failure, especially if they have been told over and over again that they ought to have sorted things out and in some hope that they can cope with change in the future.

The wider society is not clear on divorce, and is not helped by watching the church. The church might expect to know what to do more easily if divorce were a clear event in which a specific violation made it legitimate and understandable, or if it were clear what the Bible says on the matter. Divorce in the Old Testament is allowed in some cases, but not in others: yes, if a husband finds something objectionable in the wife, but not the reverse (*Deuteronomy 24:1*); no, if a woman is 'violated' because the violent man must marry the woman and is prohibited from divorcing her ever (*Deuteronomy 22:29*); no, if a man and virgin woman marry, have intercourse, and the husband pretends she was not a virgin, as he must be punished and remain with her; then yes, if she was found not to be a virgin, as she would then deserve stoning to death (*Deuteronomy 22:13ff*). Malachi prophesies that God hates divorce in the same way as he hates the covering of ones garments with violence. Hardly coherent messages.

In the New Testament, Matthew quotes Jesus as saying Moses allowed divorce because people were hard; the creation tale of the two becoming one flesh should be honoured with no one separating what God has joined. Yet Jesus says, 'if a man divorce his wife for anything other than unchastity ...', indicating that in the case of unchastity, divorce is allowed if initiated by the man. The divorced wife of this passage if remarried, however, implicates her new husband in adultery by virtue of her first marriage. Paul, who says that marriage is necessary to control the flesh, says divorce is acceptable in the case of an unbelieving spouse. He concludes, 'it is to peace that God has called you.' (*I Corinthians 7:14*) The messages of Jesus and of Paul make the matter no more clear.

Divorce is predominantly raised in the Bible as a matter of the resolution of adultery. Except for Mosaic permission for a man to divorce his wife if he doesn't like her, there is no other instance of divorce discussed. Even marriage is not defined well as it is often mentioned in the Old Testament as the making of political alliances and mentioned in the New Testament as the joining or the controlling of flesh. Marriage is not biblically clear as an institution; perhaps it is not surprising that it is difficult to discover if and how it may end.

If the matter were just adultery and then justified divorce, the clear doctrine of forgiveness present in Jesus Christ as Word made Flesh for the salvation and reconciliation of the world would mean that, even if we did see divorce as sin, it would be a forgivable sin. The only unforgivable sin raised in the Bible is sin against the Holy Spirit and I cannot even think how divorce could be this. If a forgivable sin has occurred, then the forgiven divorced people could again be in Church. Some churches do practice this, receiving people into communion and conducting second marriages, and some do not. Highly confusing in churches and out of them.

The adultery/divorce/forgiveness attitude, however, sees divorce as only the justifiable result of a sinfully betrayed relationship. Not even beginning to consider the understanding of true forgiveness between a couple as a response to adultery, this attitude assumes that divorce is always the result of a specific sin which can be forgiven. Remembering Jesus' words in Matthew, perhaps we should ask whether the two actually became 'one flesh' in the first place. Perhaps we could question whether God had actually joined the relationship. Could these be acceptable grounds for divorce? For many people the covenant-breaking act of divorce is not as a run away from sin or as a carefully defined loss in terms of scriptural imperatives, but is a positive move in faith resulting in growth, wholeness and liberation. Divorce can be the exodus event of leading out of something which is visibly or invisibly oppressive to the promised land of honesty, self knowledge, and strengthening, not weakening, of family.

Creator, Word and Lover God has been most present with me as I went through my own covenant breaking act. My faith deepened as I understood God in flesh who shared my pain. My pain was not the tangible pain of abuse or other violence; the pain was the shattering of my dreams, the shock that I had been lying to myself for so long, the visible decline in my husband's love for me and the realisation that there was something I could not fix. The more I truthfully saw and raised with my partner, the more I experienced the presence of God without understanding why. If the Church says separation is wrong, if the Bible says divorce is adulterous and sinful, then how was my faith becoming deeper? I dismissed my local Church's positive support during the divorce by seeing it as unjustified sorrow for me. I wanted them to see my fault, sin and guilt. But all I received from Christians I knew was love and all I knew from God was the love I experienced in people. Where was the judgement and the damnation?

I believe there was no judgement or damnation because the divorce was actually what my husband and I needed to grow and become as whole people as possible. Rather than being a sin about which we needed forgiveness, divorce is what we needed to become people who could live in community with others. Divorce is what we needed to be good parents to our children. Divorce is what allowed reconciliation between members of our families. Divorce gave us freedom from our self and society imposed oppression. It gave us honesty if we were willing to have it.

This is where I believe God is; in honesty, and recognition and acceptance of that honesty. In the story of Zaccheus, a man can see the truth of his life and come to a new life through the experience with Jesus. The Samaritan woman at the well is accepted by Jesus in the whole truth of her life and is the bearer of good news to her friends and relations. So many of the healing miracles are after the people to be healed come to truth. With Jesus who is the truth and the life, I cannot reconcile relationships maintained in dishonesty in order to avoid breaking covenants. Surely, that each person should live in just freedom in relationship with community, is the result of a society transformed by Christ. Where partners are unjust or dishonest, where families are forced to remain together for the sake of the neighbours' comments, where children experience violence and distrust at the hands of parents who feel threatened themselves or who are being martyrs, where all a family subsumes feeling for the sake of the institution, where there is no love bringing resurrection life or hope ... I do not see the way, the truth and the life. A marriage at any cost seems only to damage marriage partners, parents, children and extended families. It is the slavish attention to the institution without regard to human life which, to me, requires forgiveness.

With deep Christianity, we hope people will understand how to live through Good Friday after Good Friday knowing profoundly that resurrection and reconciliation with the community are the result. If families can experience the honesty of a broken covenant and the resultant resurrection event of reconciliation within the family, then the family is stronger than any tenaciously held legal bond. The reconciliation is bonded by forgiveness; not forgiveness for some definable offence, but forgiveness that the relationship did not work as a marriage and that a covenant was broken. Forgiveness, here, is for the loss of something which was created in good faith, and for any way in which anyone participated in that loss. This requires forgiveness not just between marriage partners, but also between extended members of the family.

I know there are those who say my honesty should have been seeing the fault of my broken relationship as falling from grace during marriage, and would have considered my only appropriate action would have been to live in my marriage whatever conditions. That is what generations, in the main, have done. There are those who consider personal wholeness secondary to the duties of the institution and that personal concerns are just pastoral ones and not theological ones. Some would say that if I can treat one covenant in this way, what could I do with others? Can divorced people be trusted if they break their promises? Why should the church condone such action? I could agree with all that and say my husband was the one at fault considering the way of our divorce. I could live in reflected sympathy and behave like one bereaved at an unfair time of life.

They could, I could. But I will not. I, and others like me, have found the end of one relationship the beginning of the rest of life. I am to be trusted as much as anyone who makes promises. We can know nothing concrete about the future and we can in no circumstances ever be sure of keeping promises. We go forward in good faith, believing and working for the best, trusting God of all truth to bring us to deeper faith and community. In faith we recognise that when we need to begin again, God gives us courage to lay the broken-ness of our experience at the foot of the cross. This is no mere pastoral issue; it is the deeply theological heart of the Gospel. We can know in profound Christian conviction that we will be accepted, loved and healed. I have experienced liberation; the God of exodus and resurrection can not but understand that.

The United Reformed Church suggested service for weddings includes within the prayer before the exchange of promises the following lines:

> In repentance and in faith may they know you
> as a God of mercy and new beginnings,
> who forgives our failures,
> restores our wholeness,
> and renews our hope.

A Journey to a Christian feminist view of marriage

Ruth Clarke

Is there a Christian feminist view of marriage? I have asked myself this question and have posed it to several others whom I thought might have developed one. These included individuals, publishers and the occupants of 'women's desks' in several Churches including two in the USA. Most of them expressed mild dismay at the thought of the chapter I had been asked to write.

I claim to be a Christian feminist. What I have to offer is my own journey to my current view of marriage, whilst acknowledging that there is still a long way to go in my own thinking and in testing that thinking against the experience of others.

My journey has taken me through 34 years of marriage to one man, my life shared with him as well as experiences of my own, my reading, especially of novels, my observation of other people's marriages - and a growing awareness, which has included no theological training, of the power of the gospel of Jesus Christ.

When we married in 1959, I was eager to take my husband's name, to give up my teaching career after only two years and to move with him to wherever in the world his calling would take him. My father 'gave me away' because I wanted to please him. Raymond promised to share with me his worldly goods. The only concession to 'modern' practice was that I did not promise to 'obey'. We went on our honeymoon to a part of the country that I liked and he paid. I agreed that we should have a joint bank account and I closed mine. What had I got to lose?

In Liverpool we lived in a flat above his place of work and I regarded Raymond's world as very exciting, but I soon discovered it was not mine. I met his colleagues and his friends and I stayed at home while he was busy. I went to the bank one day only to be refused cash because my husband had not given notice in writing that I was to be able to make withdrawals from our joint account. I soon went back to part-time teaching to regain some financial independence and to feel that I was contributing something of my own to society again.

Hannah, our elder daughter, was born in Liverpool in 1961, and placed great restrictions on my movements. I had to give up my job and I was not even free to play much part in Raymond's establishment. He did defy the local tradition by taking washing to the launderette, though local women offered to do it for him. We soon acquired a washing machine! Our second daughter Charlotte was born shortly after we moved to Leeds because of a new job for Raymond. Not long after her birth I was back part-time teaching in a very demanding secondary modern school near home. One motive was financial, but the main one was my inability to cope with two small children and keep my equilibrium. Raymond was much better with them than I was, but his job kept him out for long hours. I took a job with more responsibility and because it was four miles from home I had my own old car for the first time. We started to work out a pattern of shared family and domestic duties which has developed according to circumstances ever since.

In 1970 we moved to London, again because of Raymond's new post. But this time we had agreed that I too was to work and we would choose to live within two miles of my job. This worked well and I gained promotion, eventually becoming the Head of a comprehensive school. I realised that if my semi-independent spirit had not driven me back to teaching, I would never have discovered the exciting challenges of my own working life. Alongside this I was able to play an increasing part in local church life and in the United Reformed Church at district and national levels.

I took early retirement and, for the first time, my wishes about where I wanted to work led our family decisions. I became Assistant Director at the URC's lay training centre in Windermere. We moved our main home to Cumbria and settled for a small flat in London, for the convenience of both of us. For two years before his retirement Raymond commuted between Cumbria and London. In 1988 our daughter Hannah died as the result of a cycling accident near our Cumbrian home. We had always been open and loving in family relationships and our shared grief brought us and our daughter Charlotte even closer together. From 1992-93 I served as Moderator of the General Assembly of the United Reformed Church, during which time I was accompanied on most occasions by a supportive and enabling spouse and served by Charlotte as a most competent secretary.

I have told this story because, though it is particular to one marriage, it is also very familiar, paralleling the experience of many other European Christian women. Perhaps it is exceptional in having a positive conclusion in the continuing growth of both partners within the marriage and in having survived very positively after the death of a daughter. Many other stories that started like mine have ended in separation or divorce. I think particularly of another European woman whose ordained husband was very senior in his church. The wife's expectation of her role and responsibility developed in line or a little ahead of social trends. The husband's expectation of women never changed during the thirty years that the marriage lasted before divorce. None can know what somebody will be like in thirty years time. For two people to stay together in a real marriage both partners have to grow, even if not exactly at the same pace.

Ownership in the patriarchal society

Monogamous marriage was not always the norm. There are many stories in the Bible of other modes of relationship between men and women. Monogamy developed to safeguard the man's property rights. Because his wife had sexual relationships only with him, he could pass his worldly goods onto his male heir, knowing for certain that it was his own son. The wife owned nothing. Even the goods she brought into the marriage were then owned by her husband, as were her children. She was counted as one of his possessions and in the tenth commandment she listed along with the ox and the donkey and all the other belongings. Perhaps it is surprising that this institution was not abolished when Christians got round to realising that slavery was wrong.

It was following this tradition that I was given away by my father to my husband. How could I have allowed my father to assume he had the right to give me away? A woman in not the possession of a man and should not be bought, sold or given away. *The Song of Songs* declares, 'if one offered for love all the wealth of his house, it would be utterly scorned'. In the most recent *URC Service Book* the marriage ceremony enables all members of both families to give their blessing and promise support.

It was in this same tradition that Raymond made a one-way promise to share his worldly goods with me. In 1985 the then Bishop of London, Graham Leonard, wrote

> ... in the whole of human instinct and understanding it is the
> masculine which is associated with giving and the feminine
> with receiving.[1]

Surely he must have been thinking mainly about worldly goods, as,
if one is to make a generalisation at all, it should be a recognition
of all that women have given to their husbands and sons in faithful
and never-ending practical service. Through the years of our
marriage, Raymond and I have learned to share the responsibilities
and the chores and not always according to expected gender roles.
We have some common interests which are integral to the pattern
of our married life. We have also pooled our worldly goods.

There have been few men in previous centuries who have seen
marriage as an institution for mutual support but Cranmer, himself
a married man, said that marriage existed 'for the mutual society,
help and comfort that the one ought to have of the other'. If
sharing of goods, service and support is not effective this purpose
of marriage is not fulfilled. One partner can so easily become the
bearer of all the family problems. This has often been the woman,
although the husband has made all the family decisions. But many
husbands wilt under the pressure of being expected to make all the
decisions, to lay down all the rules for family life and to supply all
the family money. Men are discovering that it is not always to their
advantage to be the sole owner, the sole provider and the 'head' of
the household.

Marriage within society

Both partners should be able both to give and to receive. But
giving and receiving are not confined only to the marriage partners
and their immediate families. Married partners and their families
exist within a wider community. Jesus said, 'You shall love your
neighbour as yourself' (*Matthew 22:39*). If a married couple care
only for one another and do not serve their neighbours, however
circumstance and opportunity allow, they are not fulfilling the
commands of Jesus and not using their gifts for the bringing about
of God's kingdom.

People in the Church and in the community have expectations of or
make assumptions about other people's marriages and family life
which are based on their own up-bringing, conditioning and
experience. These too have developed largely as a result of other

people's expectations and assumptions. In order not to be judged, one tends to conform and to live out those expectations on the surface so that much of the reality of relationships is concealed from the outside. If we could accept the premise that every family should develop its own pattern of sharing, then these often damaging judgements would not be made. No couple should expect any other couple to work out their marriage in the way that they have favoured or has favoured them.

Women and men have always had and still have a yearning for life-long loyalty and security in their relationships, but there can be a point of suffering and/or abuse beyond which neither partner should be expected to go. If a marriage ceases to be a marriage, it is better that it should finish in separation or divorce, rather than destroy one or both partners.

Alternative patterns of family life

There is much debate about what constitutes a family and who is excluded if the definitions are too narrow. The ideal of the modern, white European family still seems to be two parents in their first marriage with their own children. I used to take this ideal for granted in spite of some of the tensions I have experienced through my own life.

In other places, other times, ideas are and have been very different. There are certainly many alternative models in the Old Testament for Abraham and Sarah onwards. In practice now, in modern Europe, that 'ideal' is often lost. Marriages break, one parent is on their own with the children and new relationships are made. In many African traditions, the strength of society has been based on the caring of one another within a large, extended family. Some of these traditions still allow or even encourage polygamy, though the Christian churches are working towards monogamous marriage. Something may well be lost in the process. Certainly society will be changed and new problems will have to be faced.

More controversial, especially within the Church, are partnerships where people commit themselves to a lasting relationship without making legal and religious marriage contracts. Many choose this way, but for others, marriage is impossible, for instance when former spouses will not release them or because both partners are of the same gender. Many of these relationships are more binding than life-long legal marriages which have become destructive to one or both partners. These less conventional relationships are among other factors which may challenge the future of marriage as we know it.

Power structures and patterns of activity within nuclear families, based on tradition, age and gender, can be stultifying to all members in different ways. But if we encourage marriage partnerships where people work out their own pattern, with no presuppositions of gender-related roles, it likely that this will benefit all family members. This may be hard to achieve amongst all the social pressures on us to fulfil conventional expectations. But some families do it and each one that succeeds plays a part in changing those expectations.

There are times to be together and times to be apart, times to be away and times to be within the security of the home. A family needs space, space for noise or silence, space for friends and interests. Female and male, we are all created in God's image. This places a great responsibility on us to develop the part of that image that we are made to reflect. Then, together, we can give greater glory to God by putting the pieces alongside one another and developing reciprocity, mutuality and a deep sense of oneness.

Relationship with God - independence and interdependence

How does marriage relate to our experience of God and to the gospel of Jesus? I have been much helped by Kate McIlhagga's prayer *Kindred* for week 34 in the *Prayer handbook* for 1993

> God, our Lover,
> as husbands and wives,
> friends and partners
> grow through their love,
> learn by their mistakes,
> are united yet separate,
> so may we be dependent on you,
> be independent of you,
> and interdependent with you,
> that we may truly be
> Mother, Brother, Sister of Christ
> one kindred,
> one household of faith. [2]

As human beings in God's image, women and men have been told to be fruitful and multiply and take responsibility for our environment (*Genesis 1:26-13*). That fruitfulness includes conceiving, bearing and nurturing children, but the task is much greater than that. Each individual has been given their own particular range of gifts and a breadth of options so that they may use those gifts for the greater glory of God.

We are dependent on God for all we have, but God has given us our independence and freed us to exercise choice. We are interdependent with God in our growth in love, our spiritual and practical development and the use of our gifts. This paradox is the one reflected in marriage in the relationship between man and woman. We are independent individuals, dependent on one another for faithful love and interdependent as we support one another and share together.

Jesus advocated faithfulness within monogamy and he had no double standards for men and women. The way in which Jesus accepted women, including their sexuality, broke the taboos of the time. He acknowledged and healed illnesses associated with being female. Paul wrote in *Galatians 3:28* '... there is no longer male and female; for all of you are one in Christ Jesus'. This is a much more universal application of the whole gospel of Christ than some of his other writings which exclude women from some roles and place the position of wife as subservient to her husband. Though, even when Paul is at his 'worst' he does expect men to love and respect their wives.

Conclusion

I chose to marry - I did not have to. A Christian feminist choosing to marry clearly does not reject men! My Christian feminism is an essential aspect of my wider desire for justice. It leads me to see that married people can serve the community and bring about a greater sense of justice, including a more positive experience of personal, committed relationships.

I do not oppose marriage as an institution, but only those aspects of it that are unjust to women. I see the laws and assumptions of our own society about marriage moving in the right direction. They are moving, although too slowly, away from the kind of monogamy that exists for the benefit of men towards the expectation of a mutuality that is in accord with the Christian gospel. Marriage and other lasting and loving relationships can, in part, mirror the interdependence and independence that we can experience in our relationship with God.

---

1   From the Bishop of London's newsletter of November 1985. Quoted by Elaine Storkey in M.Furlong (ed.) *Mirror to the Church: reflections on sexism,* SPCK, 1988.

2   *Encompassing Presence,* Prayer handbook 1993, URC, 1993.

Peter's death

Janet Elizabeth Chesney

At approximately 6.00pm on 26th October, 1984, my husband, Revd Peter Chesney, had a heart attack from which he never regained consciousness. At 7.00pm the hospital gave up trying to resuscitate him and I was allowed to see him for the last time. What follows is a record of my experience of God over the next seven or so years after his death.

As 'theology' this record is almost entirely experiential because that is how I, personally, 'study' God. It is more or less in chronological order though towards the end some independent strands developed simultaneously. As such it is unique to me, but I offer it with love and with hope that it may encourage everyone who reads it to share their pain, understanding and joy with others.

As I see it, Peter's death offered me an unprecedented opportunity to begin again with my life and I have grown into a more wonderful human being than I ever dreamed possible. Perhaps I could say that he died that I might live more abundantly. In this way I can find purpose in his dying where otherwise there might appear to be none.

I begin my experiences when I went to see 'the body', to say 'Good-bye' and found myself caught up in a cosmic party ...

'I danced in the morning and I danced on the Earth'.

Waiting welcoming God, with what joy you rush out to meet us
To 'dress us in the best' and 'prepare a feast in our honour'.
God of Dance and Song, Movement and Light
What a party you give for this son who was lost and is found
Who was dead and is now alive!
Such a celebration as only Heaven can give.

A glimpse, for me, of the dynamic eternal jigsaw of creation
Where I fit exactly in my ever-changing perfect place
I am flying, whirling, laughing... at last I understand.

But earth waits now in the touch of a nurse's hand on mine
I fall, and landing breaks me into a million fragments
Kind people lead me away, silently screaming.

'Never was love ..., never was grief like Thine'

Weeping God, have you no comforting words for me
Trudging along beside me through wet Autumn leaves
Berating the sky, as I do, echoing my words
'What a waste! What a mess! What's the point?'
There is no point. No rhyme nor reason.
You offer nothing to give me hope
Nothing to relieve my pain.

I long to lay my weary head upon Your heart
And feel Your protecting arms around me.
Shield me from this unbearable madness of grief.
I am dying a lingering death
As my spirit is slowly seeping out of me.
O God comfort me!

But You just continue weeping
And as the warm tears of divine sorrow wash over me
I can at last truly experience my pain
And know myself fully alive.

'O Love that will not let me go'.

Resilient God I do not want you around
Yet You surround me with your elasticated boundary of Love.

I am ANGRY, I am ANGER, I am consumed by it.
Angry at the stupid doctor who didn't believe
That Peter was having a heart attack -
Let him walk upstairs to bed, to die.

Angry at the Church that made such demands
And often did not appreciate the cost.

Angry at Peter because he gave so much of himself to others
There was so little left for himself ... and for me.

Angry at myself because when I look back
All that I can remember are the mistakes
The misunderstandings
Why can't I remember the happy times?
Why did I feel undervalued, misused,

Forced into a role of 'wife' that I was born to
Yet despised?
Trapped by society, my background and Peter who had to be King.
And I felt powerless to change it.

I am angry at my powerlessness, my weakness.
I am a child in a tantrum
I am afraid of the violence in my anger
It fills my mind, warps my view and distorts every sound.
I want to lash out, stamp, scream
Slam, bite, rip, smash ...

Resilient God, your love stretches, but never breaks.

'Out of the depths I cry to Thee'

Deep Dark God, You are amazing to me.
So long have I wallowed and struggled
Through this mud of despair.
Blinded, deafened, disorientated
By the suffocating slime of hopelessness,
Believing You to be a goading God
Prodding and poking me to keep me going
When I wanted to give up.

Through the long days and weeks of darkness
I wrestled,
Trying to reach the Light
To find You.

This morning, energy, hope, fear, everything gone
I gave up.

Into the emptiness a voice whispered,
 'The darkness is also God'
 'As we forgive those who trespass against us'

Reconciling, reuniting God, You release me
From the cage of unforgiveness
Beckoning me to those whom I have hurt
And who have hurt me.

I do not want to face them
It is easier to wrap myself in the cold blankets
Of guilt and resentment
Than look them in the eye.
Easier to pretend they don't exist
Or that it is not possible to do anything about them.

Your gentle loving touch lifts my chin
And I see Peter waiting.
Waiting to say 'I'm sorry, please forgive me.
You hurt me, too, but I want to forgive you.'

I am in turmoil, my emotions run riot
I am afraid of him, I love him,
I am angry with him, he is my friend,
He is my tormentor, my lover, my jailer
I want to punish him, I want to forgive him
I want to live my life without him
But he hangs around my neck like rotting meat.

With trembling hands I lay my burden at his feet
He lays his at mine
With trembling hearts we begin unpacking piece by piece.
So many words left unsaid
So many feelings left unexpressed.
Tears flow as we realise it was all so unnecessary.

Slowly the pieces dissolve, going into the earth
Transformed to rich compost from which true loving can grow
I forgive, I am forgiven.

It is time to love, it is time to laugh.
When was the last time I really laughed?
'Remember the time ...?' I laugh.
Yes we were happy, there are happy memories.
Time to stick them in the scrapbook of life
And put them away with my other treasures
To be taken out and enjoyed at will.

Time to let the other memories go, to clear the air.
To walk forward lightly in my forgiveness
'Good-bye Peter', now I can let you go.
Who knows if we shall be together
In another time, another space?
It will be better then because of this.

Atoning God, You enable us to become at one
In your eternity
One with ourselves, with other human beings
And with all creation.

'Make me a channel of Your Peace'

Plumber God, You come to clear the blocked drains of my life.
So many unfulfilled needs from childhood
So many incorrect beliefs about myself
My world and about You
Prevent the flow of Your energy and love through me.

So many unexpressed emotions
Stuffed into the old carrier bags of my life
So much effort needed
To keep them tightly closed.

But blocked drains and unwashed rags cause smells
My life is turning sour,
Gently Your love reaches in
Persuades me to let go.
The pain is extreme
I scream,
I bleed,
Will I survive?

But at last healing is possible.
Eventually I begin to feel myself opening
To receive Your wisdom.
Slowly understanding dawns:
This is what giving up the self is all about
Finding the real self; vibrant with love
Free flowing through me.

Dynamic God, painstakingly You make me whole.

**'O hush the noise ye men of strife
And hear the angels sing'**

'Masculine, Male God. Powerful and Triumphant
How I hate the macho images given You by man.
Man? Men. Men and women in cahoots
To show masculine rules over feminine
Three-fold Male God?
The mind boggles, the heart grieves
And my spirit is bowed
By the weight of such Strength and Might.

I feel trampled underfoot, unnoticed
By a man willing to lay down his life.
Willing to die, like men in war, heroically
Among the filth and pain of needless suffering.

Twisted truths and outright lies have produced
Grotesque distortions of a gentle, compassionate God
Trumpets sounding victory drown
The words of acceptance and forgiveness
From a truly loving human being
Revealing the divine.

I looked for bread and was given a snake
Punitive, warmongering, conquering god
I denounce you, I will have no more of you.

**'Mother-like She tends and spares us
Well our feeble frame She knows
In Her hands She gently bears us'**

Feminine, Female God, nurturing and encouraging
Where are the images of Mother, She and Her?
Where are you
In your willingness to live, not die,
To live and share among the filth and pain
Of needless suffering?

How am I made in the image
Of a masculine image of God?

For too long the 'masculine' part of me
Ruled over the 'feminine' part.
Despised the softness, emotion, intuition, wisdom
In favour of the bully, the tom-boy
The 'brave' well-armoured front.

No more.

I come into Your presence
And do not fall at Your feet, a sinner,
But am lifted up!
I see myself as I really am
Made in the image of God at last
A truly magnificent, loving woman.

Unknown, unimaginable God, set me free;
Free from all images of gender, race or creed.
Free, even, from the search
To find images of You.

Free to float in the vastness beyond mind
Beyond thought, beyond wildest imaginings
To feel the frightening mystery of the unknown.

Territory without directions or map
No track, no road, for travellers to find
No near, no far, no-one knows the way.
Here is no way -
Only the spirit of adventure in each of us
That rejoices to experience:

The limitlessness of God ...
 in a sparkling drop of dew
The minute part of God ...
 that forms our Universe.

Gone are the boundaries of form and space and time
All is one, the alpha and the omega
As I return to be the part of God
That I have always been.

Marriage matters

Brian Haymes

Marriage has traditionally involved the union of a woman and a man, mutually and freely undertaken in life long commitment, publicly witnessed, and sexually consummated. Such a definition is stark, cold and open to several qualifications and objections but the fact is that such an understanding of marriage has been around for a very long time. Some have argued that it is in the 'nature' of things. But what is natural is not easy to pin down and traditions are revised. What seemed so right and proper can be viewed under different circumstances as painfully wrong. Certainly contemporary Christians in Britain are having to face sharp questions about the meaning and practice of marriage both from without and within the Church. Not that there ever has been one clear doctrine of marriage held by all Christians. For example, speaking very generally, the Orthodox churches, with their more positive appreciation of God's joy in creation have grounded their understanding of marriage in the doctrine of a positively good creation. They have had a more open attitude to divorce and remarriage. Human sexuality has been decidedly affirmed and priests have not been required to be celibate.

Within the western churches of the Roman discipline, being dominated for much of their history by doctrines of sin and redemption often cast in legal categories, marriage has been seen as a sacrament within the divinely decreed and authorized means of grace. The doctrine of creation is not forgotten, of course, but the shadow of Augustine's rather negative view of our sexuality still darkens the sky and we are not free of it yet. In these western churches the doctrine of the indissolubility of marriage has resulted in an almost totally negative view being taken of divorce.

The Reformed tradition can serve as a third example. Here the sacramental view of marriage has been down-played against a more contractual perspective. Marriage was understood less as an ecclesiastical event than as a basic order of creation. Calvin and Luther both acknowledged the reality of divorce, not the least because they found it in the Bible.

Thus Christians have understood marriage in different ways, or at least from different perspectives. This has been the case and probably always will be. What particular factors and emphases might be part of Christian reflections on marriage today?

First, there is sense in understanding marriage in terms of creation. The institution has a very long history. There were marriages long before there were Christians. *Mark 10:1–9* seems to suggest that creation is where marriage belongs. As such, Jesus did not found 'Christian marriage' but drew attention to its place in creation. Marriage belongs, in this sense, in the 'natural order'. And given that the doctrine of creation is not so much about a 'one-off' divine event but has more to do with God's continuing work, then marriage might be seen as an important collaborative response by those called to this kind of partnership. Into marriage God calls his daughters and sons, with their own freedom to co-operate with or frustrate the divine creative purpose. It is not without interest, given this perspective, that we have come to talk about 'making' love, creating and expressing the unity in plurality which is a feature of God's creation.

Thus marriage might be seen as a divine possibility for humankind. Marriage is 'made', not by the religious officials, attitudes or actions, but by the partners in consent. People 'marry' each other. Any official present may help the ceremony along but acts mainly like all others present as witnesses to this further expression of creation which itself may lead, potentially, to further creativity. As Helen Oppenheimer has put it, the 'one flesh' union in marriage is not an odd thing to find in this universe if Christianity is the truth.[1]

This emphasis on the positive virtue, enjoyment and creativity of marriage needs to be asserted against some negative attitudes found in the western world. It may be that Augustine has been over-harshly treated and has not deserved all that has been attributed to him but he could not get out of his head and his teaching a connection between sex and sin. He believed that the origin of the sexual act in a fallen world was male lust. Therefore all sexual acts are sinful. It may not be strictly true to charge him with teaching that 'original sin' was passed on in the very act of sexual intercourse as some have suggested but he did believe that it was in sin that his mother conceived him and that is the case with all of us. Sex, for all its place in the divine creation, was all right for Augustine as long as your intention was procreation and that you did not enjoy it!

This negative attitude to our sexuality has done immeasurable harm and remains with us to this day. It concentrates on the depravity of humankind, not the possibilities of sharing in God's good creative purposes. Original sin is such a dark cloud that we can lose sight of any abiding original righteousness.

Increasingly a more positive attitude is being taken towards our sexuality. References to the 'remedy for sin' in marriage services have disappeared. A deeper appreciation of the creative work of God and our partnership with God has enriched our understanding of marriage.

A further area of reflection has to do with what were called the 'ends' of marriage. Traditionally these were threefold; procreation, 'remedy for sin' and caring companionship. What has happened is that, increasingly, the third element, of companionship, has become most significant. The influential Church of England report on marriage and divorce, *Putting asunder,*[2] argued that divorce should be possible where a marriage, as a living relationship, had irretrievably broken down. The notion of 'irretrievability' is hard to define but clearly the quality of relationship between the partners is a crucial factor in any marriage. A marriage in name only is no more a marriage than a nominal Manchester United supporter is the real thing.

The emphasis on the quality of the relationship in marriage has been reflected in changes in divorce laws in England. Divorce has become easier, quicker and much less socially important than was the case. At the same time the number of those co-habiting has increased. This raises questions about what actually does constitute a marriage. The emphasis on the quality of relationship has overshadowed other factors, such as procreation and social recognition. What place do these have in an understanding of marriage or is the quality of relationship to carry the whole weight?

Marriage, however it is understood, takes place in a social context and a number of important non-theological factors have had their effect on the English scene. The industrial revolution brought with it a rapid increase in urban life. People moved to the towns and such mobility meant social change for the family and marriage.

The extended family, with all its supportive networks, was one casualty, increasingly so as more people moved with their work. The experience of family changed and the nuclear family came to be. It is more than likely that in small, pre-industrial immobile communities some marriages were virtually arranged. With social mobility a wider choice of possible partners was available.

The nuclear family on the move meant a potential social isolation in their self-sufficient little house and, in particular, a greater loneliness for women. Earlier social assumptions were that women bore and nurtured the children while attending to domestic matters. Slowly traditional 'roles' have been challenged (many would say with hardly any real change at all) but increasingly some marriages have come to be seen more as a partnership with assumed roles being less and less clear. There can be little doubt that for many women marriage has been and remains a frustratingly limited world. And all this has happened while, at the same time, the human resources of extended families have become less available. A further factor to be reckoned with is increasing longevity which means that life-long commitments to care and faithfulness encounter more stress than before.

One other factor that has had virtually revolutionary consequences has been the availability of virtually safe contraception. Children are now 'planned' and 'made'. In consequence, families are smaller. Indeed a marriage may be childless by decision, in direct challenge to the traditional 'ends'. Both inside and outside marriage sex can be free of the fear of pregnancy. Some of the sexual morality of the past was undoubtedly based on fear. A new climate has been created. Our Victorian grand-parents seemed to have been over-obsessed with death while sex was a taboo subject. We have reversed that for sex is a regular topic while death is the great unmentionable.

Such social changes as these have certainly affected how we look at marriage and Christians have not been able to live outside this revolution however much some may have wished to do so. Indeed many of us would not want to live outside these changes because they have hardly been all bad. However, among the consequences of these changes there are two that seriously challenge the Christian traditions of marriage.

The first is that of divorce and remarriage. The divorce rate has risen sharply. Does this, of itself, mean a lower or higher quality of married life? Much of the western tradition of marriage was shaped by legalistic categories such as indissolubility. In earlier generations to be divorced was to be disgraced. Just how much mental, physical and spiritual agony this policy caused is impossible to quantify. There is an argument, often heard, that the increasing divorce rate and the breakdown of family life undermines society and its well-being. Family life and marriage are taken to be part of the divine ordering of the world and necessary for a stable society. But even if this debatable argument is true, to insist, on that basis, that people have to stay in bad marriages, where fundamental relationships have broken down and those involved are being diminished as people, is to confuse legalism and pastoral care. We do not promote the institution of marriage by legalistically insisting on the continuance of bad ones.

It is frequently asserted that divorce, in legal terms, has become too easy. But it might be argued that, because of the emphasis on the centrality of relationships, it is marriage that has become too easy, with not enough preparation and all too little support for those within it. Such support might well have been given in years past by the local extended family. Jack Dominion, Director of the Marriage Research Centre, has been insisting for some time that the churches should back more research into what actually is happening in and to marriage and how couples might receive more support and preparation.[3]

If the open attitude to relationships and divorce and remarriage is taken what of the remarriage of divorcees in church? Would such an act compromise the Christian teaching on marriage as being 'for life' quite out of existence? Generally speaking Christians would have to acknowledge that, as far as we know his mind, Jesus of Nazareth was against divorce. That needs to be recorded because it reminds us that this is a serious question for the Christian Church.

However, Christians might well argue that the Church must be creative and ready to take risks and be prepared to help those who have been divorced to make a new marriage. This is to challenge the tradition but Christians of all people ought to be able to acknowledge that the ideals are often beyond us, imperfect as we are, and that mistakes are made. In the real world some people rush into marriage unwisely, some marriages hardly live at all and

some are still-born from the start. There are fearful situations
where one partner's heart is broken because they really do love
the other who no longer has any love for them. People can be
destroyed by such unreciprocated loving. It may be possible for
the divine love to continue though it be unloved, as in Hosea 11,
but that is beyond most of us. In such tragic circumstances,
recognising our human frailty, the pastoral challenge may be in
helping people through their sorrow and pain, their sense of guilt
and failure, and, in the name of God, to help them have the courage
to make new relationships, even to the extent of a new commitment
in marriage.

There are obviously difficult questions here about criteria of
judgement in cases. An open policy for all comers without
qualification is not being advocated. A too liberal approach is no
better than never allowing the question at all. As human beings
we have to live with these difficult moral choices.

A further challenge to the tradition comes from those who choose
to cohabit, either for a brief while prior to marriage, or as
permanent common law marriages. Some still speak of 'trial'
marriages but since the heart of marriage is commitment it is
hardly a 'marriage' if the understanding is that any partner can
drop out at will. An obviously important question is to what extent
any marriage is a social as well as personal event. No couple lives
entirely to themselves but how far is social, even lawful,
recognition necessary? A report written by Duncan Dormor for
One Plus One: Marriage And Partnership Research (Central
Middlesex Hospital) entitled *The relationship revolution* argues
that by the turn of the century four out of five couples getting
married in England and Wales will have lived together before.
Up to half those getting married at present have cohabited and the
reason for marriage is starting a family. It is likely that the number
of children brought up by one parent will increase because of the
frailty of relationships.

It might be argued that a marriage formally and legally contracted
in Church or Registry Office, but where the relationship has
virtually collapsed, is a marriage but deficient. It is deficient,
not in its formal, legal, social aspects but in the quality of its
relationship. Again, a common law marriage, strong in relationship
but with no formal public standing is a marriage but deficient. Its
deficiency lies in lack of social awareness, a marriage being more

than two people doing their own thing. The personal emphasis on relationship must not so dominate that the social aspects of marriage are totally abandoned. There is something to the assertion that society needs good order, not the least for the sake of children and the responsibility owed them.

The situation we are in is far from clear and changing all the time. What shall Christians say to a rising generation about marriage?

First, we have to affirm the Christian understanding of love as the basis for all life and not just that of marriage. It is within marriage and family, though not exclusively so, that many of us find the reality of love and therefore of God. Christians will always speak of love in terms of Christ, of faithfulness to friends, of sacrifice for their sakes, of personal fulfilment in God's purposes. As Stanley Hauerwas says, 'the Christian tradition claims that marriage helps to support an inclusive community of love by grounding it in a pattern of faithfulness towards each other.'[4] Love defined as *agape* will always be subversive of the general human response but it is at the centre of true community of which marriage is one important expression.

A significant factor contributing to our present problems is the fact that any quality of trust between people is itself based on a shared moral foundation. If we give one another our word that we shall be faithful that is only so strong as our conviction that promise keeping is a claim made on both of us. For Christians, the promises made before God are of this character. Both parties to the marriage know God's claim on their lives and their life together. There is an old paradox here which is important and liberating because the acknowledgement of this claim of another is the ground of genuine freedom. In marriage it is also true that the individual who wants to save her or his life must lose it in the other. And Christians would say, together in God. Such love is the ground of freedom. It is indeed subversive of an attitude that seeks only personal satisfaction and owns no claim to a greater loyalty than one's own desires.

Second, let Christians speak positively and honestly about human sexuality. Sexual relations are not something that happens apart from the rest of ourselves. Because of the deep unity of our minds, emotions, personality and body, all sexual relations are precious, personal and costly. They are properly at home in the kind of

committed faithfulness that marriage is. Casualness with ourselves
and other people, at any level of our life is unwise.

Why unwise? Not because of possibly pregnancy or disease,
that old morality of fearfulness that once was pressed on us, but
because of the fact that what happens in the body happens to the
person. We need to assert the value of each person, that it is
important to care for one's self, that whereas sexuality in
commitment remains one of life's glories, being so high it can sink
so low. People can and do get badly hurt. The deepest springs of
our being are being touched. That is why sex can be so wonderful
and holy. That is why it is one of the ways God draws near and we
find grace in the midst of life. We might expect that 'making love'
engages with God.

But the nature of the divine love is that it is always 'going out' of
itself, to others, to creation. So we might understand not simply
that a marriage is the appropriate context for a child but that the
very bringing of a child into being is properly an act of love.
Those who are in love now, of their love, seek to bring a new life
into being. The birth of a child, any child, is a great moment in the
history of our humanity. The child expresses something of the
divine hope for us and commitment to us. That a child might know
this kind of love in shared commitment is to see each family as a
parable of the kingdom. It is to suggest that, for all the cruel
distortions we may bring to it, marriage matters.

1   See her article on 'Marriage' in the *New Dictionary of Christian ethics,* SCM
    Press.
2   SPCK, 1966.
3   See his *Passionate and Compassionate Love,* Darton, Longman and Todd, 1991.
4   S. Hauerwas, *After Christendom?,* Abingdon, 1991.

Marriage address

Colin Gunton

In Somerset House, where once were lodged all the records of
births, marriages and deaths, there is now the Courtauld Institute of
Art. When the gallery moved to its new home, a year or two ago, it
put out a series of posters, based on paintings in its collection, to
encourage people to visit it. On one of them were the words:
'Visit Somerset House to find out about your ancestors' and the
accompanying painting was, of course, one of Adam and Eve in the
Garden of Eden. Why does that ancient story, coming from the
dawn of human history, still appeal so much to the imagination?
Even the silly jokes and stories that gather round it witness to its
continuing fascination. The answer, of course, has largely to do
with the part it, along with all the Bible, has played in our history.
So many echoes and resonances of scripture go very deep into our
ways of speech and thought. But another reason is that the story
contains a profound meditation on the human condition.

If we are to appreciate its profundity, we must understand it for
what it is. It is not science, it is not history, but rather what
Coleridge called a living educt of the imagination; a picture which
lives because, generation after generation, it opens up to us
dimensions of our being that would otherwise remain quite hidden.
Without such stories we would not know who we are - as, of
course, in our strange lost modern world we often do not. One
aspect of its appeal to the imagination is that it asks us to imagine
man - for Adam in Hebrew simply means man - alone, or rather,
and this is the key to the story, with the company only of the
animal kingdom. And the story is quite clear; none of the animals
is his equal, able to provide him with the companionship he needs -
not even the faithful English dog. None of them can provide the
true counterpart, the one who must be there is he is to be truly
himself. And so God makes Eve, woman. Notice that God takes
here from Adam's side, so that she is not his inferior, not his
superior, but one who is to be genuinely beside him, as different,
but as a true companion. And the cry of joy with which he greets
Eve when he awakes is testimony to the wonder of it all. 'This at
last is bone of my bones, and flesh of my flesh.' And the writer
comments: 'Therefore a man leaves his father and mother and
cleaves to his wife, and they become one flesh.'

As you will know, the story goes on to tell of other things, of what happens when human relationships go sour. We have to face the fact that that, too, is part of our human condition, only too much in evidence from the deep unhappiness that marks so many lives. It teaches us that the man-woman relationship is the most difficult and dangerous feature of our human condition. But that is not the thing with which we are concerned this happy day. The man-woman relationship is the most difficult because it is the most necessary, rewarding and promising aspect of our being. The most satisfying things about our lives are not those that come easily, at the turn of a switch, or the press of a remote control button. They are the things that take time; that have to be built patiently, year after year, with thought, pain, loyalty and above all love. That is something you, Peter and Carolyn, know already, but you will go on learning. The best human achievements take time; in this case, a lifetime:

> love which lasts when youth has faded,
> bends with age, but never dies.

As the centre of all other relationships, marriage is at once the most private and the most public of all our institutions. It is the most private because there are some things about it which ought never to be shared, some things which are between husband and wife alone as they grow together, make a home and raise a family. I am sometimes shocked when I hear people making public and sometimes disparaging remarks about their spouses, airing things that are clearly private and ought to remain so. In the things that belong to two people alone, a private space is necessary for love and loyalty to develop and to cement so crucial a relationship. There we come again to that comment of the writer of the story of Adam and Eve: 'they shall become one flesh'.

What is the meaning of this mysterious but very direct, almost indelicate sounding, expression? Let me say first what it does not mean; that there should be in the marriage relationship a merging of personalities, or the subordination of one to the other. That is the opposite of what is meant. In my view, the most important, if also most difficult, thing to achieve in a marriage is a pattern of relationships in which husband and wife enable each other to be themselves, to grow into the unique human being that we are all meant to be. The positive meaning of the 'one flesh' is to be found in the comment which precedes it in the text. 'Therefore a man leaves his father and mother and cleaves to his wife ...' That gives us not only an interesting insight into Hebrew relationships - notice that it is the man who has to do the moving - but also the key to the general matter that we are seeking. When we are young, our relationship with our parents is the one that shapes our being, is most important in making us who we are. Now it is the relationship of husband and wife that comes into the centre. You will remain the children of the four parents who are so delighted to be sharing in this day, but your relationship to each other will now be the one which centrally defines who you are, the one in which you are called to grow in love for each other and in responsibility to the rest of the community.

Marriage is not only the most private but also the most public of institutions, and for a number of reasons. First, it is that on which the health of our social order depends. It is not only that without it the human race would die out; that is obvious, though it needs saying. It is also that from it flow all the other things that are necessary for the life in community without which we cannot be ourselves. Without good and secure marriages, all our social institutions are at risk. More positively, get things right here and the rest will, for the most part, look after themselves. That is not to say that other things do not matter, but that they begin here. According to Coleridge, personal affections expand 'like the circles of a Lake - the Love of our Friends, parents and neighbours leads us to the love of Country to the love of all Mankind.' That has an old-fashioned air, but it is true. There is a well known cartoon in which one of the Peanuts characters says, 'I love humanity. It's people I can't stand.' The testing and private places, not only marriage but all our close friendships, provide the learning grounds for the wider sympathies which are so desperately needed outside the inner circles of affection.

Marriage is a public institution for the second reason that without public acknowledgement and support, its very privacy will turn in upon itself and die. As theologians have sometimes said, true love needs at least a third if it is not to turn dangerously in upon itself. Although there will be those blessed times when there are just the two of you and no more - and you will need them - without children and parents, brothers, sisters, aunts, uncles and the rest, without neighbours and friends, without the company of the human beings that God throws across our road, in all their loveable and irritating ways, any human relationship is poorer than it might be.

What our story tells us is that God has made us not for ourselves, but for each other. And that is why occasions of this kind are so important. It is not that marriages are necessarily better for going through all the traditional forms, though they may well be. It is rather that a marriage is one of the inner circles of the lake of humankind, and the outer circles have an interest in it. They are affected by it and, more important, they are called to give support to it in whatever way they are called to do. Those of us who are privileged to be here are here because marriage is and must be a public as well as a private affair. And that means that we are called to support Carolyn and Peter in the way each of us best can in the high and holy calling which they are entering.

I began this address with a reference to that old story of Adam alone in the garden. It would be wrong to end it without reference to the second Adam who went to another garden, alone and without the blessings of human support. It is there, in the Word of God made flesh for us, that we see our human loves, with all their inadequacies and weaknesses, embraced within the love that moves the stars. It is that above all that we come to celebrate today; that we can love, because we have loved. That is not a magic formula for success in life, but if your remember that during your marriage, you won't go far wrong. God bless you.

This sermon was preached at the wedding of Peter Evans and Carolyn Gunton. The biblical story to which it refers is found in *Genesis 2*.

Towards healthy marriage

Peter Rand

Marriage is the closest relationship any of us choose to have. It is 'the relationship from which we, at times, want to break out, and yet the one to which we are longingly drawn back'.[1] A good marriage provides good things for the two people in it - physical and emotional security, role, social position. At its best marriage provides the place where partners can discover themselves and grow as individuals, and help each other to do the same. To be compared with the joys of parenting, this experience of growing and helping another to grow in marriage is probably one of life's most rewarding experiences.

However, a poor marriage can be a destructive experience. Rather than a safe place in which to grow, it can be a trap in which to be suffocated. The damage may extend to the children and outwards into family and society. And it is not confined to those marriages which end in divorce. I have spoken to people who, in their thirties and forties and later, suffer from the insecurity which began with parents who were unhappy together but stayed together 'for the children'.

Jesus said 'I have come that you might have life - life in all its fullness' (*John 10.10* GNB). And Jesus spent much of his time giving health - physical, emotional, spiritual. In the same way, the Christian Church, which, as Paul says, is the Body of Christ (*I Corinthians 12.27*), is in the business of the provision of health - physical, emotional and spiritual.

The title of this chapter is *Towards Healthy Marriage*. It seeks to look more closely at the task of Christians in 'health promotion' in the area of marriage.

If we are to promote healthy marriage, we must relate to people, and before we can relate to people fully, we must accept them as they are. Very often I find myself in conflict with good Christian people who are much too ready to judge others. They say things like: 'How can people promise to stay together 'till death do us part' when they've already promised the same thing to someone else and broken their promise?' They say that when divorce and remarriage are allowed, the fabric of society is weakened. They say that when clergy are too ready to give understanding to those whose marriages have broken up, they undermine the efforts of those who struggle to keep their marriages whole, and who uphold the ideal of lifelong commitment 'for better or worse'.

Comments like these hold much truth. But I believe that this truth must be balanced against the needs of individuals. And this is where I bring in the Bible. For it seems to me that the attitude of Jesus was one of acceptance, and the offering of a relationship. I choose two stories in particular. They both involve women who have led less than blameless lives (I am not sure why men in the gospels never come in for criticism because of their sexual morals!). The first is the woman Jesus met by the well at Sychar (*John 4*). After the conversation about the water of life, when the woman asked for this water, Jesus told her to fetch her husband. She told a white lie, saying that she had no husband, to which Jesus replied 'No, you're right, you've had five, and the man you're living with isn't your husband really'. Some commentators suggest that there is some moral superiority in Jesus' tone here. But even if it is there, it does not prevent Jesus from accepting the woman. He is open to her and to her needs. He forms a relationship with her within which he can attend to her and assist her to bring about change in her life. The second of these women was the woman caught in the act of adultery (*John 8*). Here, the fact that Jesus did not approve of her conduct is much clearer. He did not try to stop the stone-throwers on the grounds that their action was unlawful - they were putting into practice the due punishment for crime, and Jesus did not contradict that. Neither did he condone what the woman had done. On the contrary, he used the word 'sin' of the woman's conduct. But he accepted her as a person. Only when he had said to her 'I do not condemn you' did he go on to say 'Go, and don't sin any more.'

Just as Jesus accepted people as they were, so, I believe, Christians should accept people. If we are to help people to form good relationships, if we are to promote healthy marriages, then first we must be ready to form relationships with people based on acceptance of them, with all their faults and weaknesses. For, let us not forget that we, like those who were going to throw the stones, are not without sin either.

I recognise that this poses a problem. How do we uphold ideals while accepting people who have fallen short of those ideals? It is not easy. It is a tightrope which I believe we are called by God to walk. He does not give us easy answers.

If we in the church are to re-examine the biblical material and established ethical principles related to marriage, a new look at the theology of marriage is called for. As a pastor and counsellor I would like to plead for a change. For too long our understanding of humankind has been that we are 'individuals'. But is that how God sees us? Our doctrine of the Trinity sees God as 'three persons in relation to one another':

> Creator God
> Father, Son and Spirit ...
> ...
> let your Spirit speak
> of your Son's sacrifice
> and of your Father's love.[2]

Note the 'your' in each line - each person of the Trinity is related to the others and each is in a real sense incomplete without the others. Similarly, we as human beings are incomplete without one another. We are not whole when we are individuals, we become whole when we become 'persons in relation'. Anyone who has been in love knows this. But in a good marriage this 'making someone else whole' goes beyond 'love's young dream'. It is a lifelong commitment, task and adventure. Psychologists have long recognised the value of committed relationships for healing people's emotional wounds. Theologians need to recognise it too and not just for healing wounds, but as the place in which people can grow into what God meant them to be. For we are who we are by virtue of our relationships with others. So, we can value marriage not just as an instrument for keeping people virtuous but as a place in which we become what we truly are, what God wills us to be, and in which we find God's grace touching us and giving us liberation. This prayer, from a marriage service, suggests this.

> Gracious God, always faithful in your love for us ...
> ...You create love
> and out of loneliness
> unite us in one human family

... make new the lives of A and B whose marriage we celebrate.
Bless all creation
through the sign of your love
given in their love for each other.[3]

We need more positive images of marriage. Much can and should
be done to recover the ideal of lifelong commitment. It has been
said that we live in the 'throw-away society'. I have heard couples
preparing for marriage say, 'we'll get married and if it doesn't
work out we'll get divorced'. This attitude can only weaken the
commitment of the partners to each other and lessen the chance of
working through the difficulties which may arise in their marriage.
The media, particularly television, can help by showing the joy that
comes through wrestling with painful issues and 'coming through,
scarred but together'. More emphasis needs to be put on the pain
of failure in relationships, to counter the view that divorce is easy.
These ideas may seem naive, but they are more helpful and
constructive than seeing marriage as good only as long the
partners are 'happy' in a romantic way. Currently there is an
ecumenical Media Awareness Project which has these, among
others, as its aims.

There is much to be done in helping young people to understand
more about relationships. A look at the magazines produced for
teenagers and especially at the 'agony' pages, shows that young
people are wanting to find out and understand how relationships
work and how to make them work better. These same pages
suggest how difficult young people find this. I wonder if this is
due, in part, to the pressure they are under from those same media;
pressure to form relationships before they are ready, pressure to be
'successful' with the opposite sex. Some time ago, I had occasion
to talk to some young women of 16-20 years old, and this subject
came up. I asked them whether they thought it would be a good
thing to go into schools and talk to people in the 3rd, 4th and 5th
years about issues surrounding relationships. I was expecting
blank looks, but they were very enthusiastic, wondered why it had
never been done before, and gave me a list of topics they thought
ought to be included!

Some teachers and church workers are already working on this. It
is not an easy area. Sex, particularly, is difficult to discuss - the
young people are naturally embarrassed and many teachers too.
There is a need for specialist training to help teachers deal with the

issues in the most helpful way possible. Some Relate centres have taken an initiative by putting on courses for teachers and others on the subject of 'Talking about Sex'. Perhaps teaching on relationships could be shared between teachers and others in the community - ministers, counsellors, health professionals and people who simply bring their own experience of relationships.

Once people get to the point of marriage there is more work to be done. People are 'prepared' for marriage by seeing their own parents' marriage and by their own experience of family life. For many this is a very good preparation, where communication is good and each individual is valued. However every family is different and when two people come together to get married, they bring with them their different ideas about what 'family' means - expectations about roles, standards, habits and so on. In a marriage preparation course I help to run, we do a role play of an engaged couple shopping - she wants to buy a hot water bottle and he doesn't. In her family, it is part of the bedtime ritual to fill hot water bottles, make cocoa etc. In his family, fitness is the order of the day (and evening) - with cold beds to encourage the circulation and bedroom windows open at night for fresh air. This may seem trivial, but this kind of difference can easily cause friction and heartache. This is true even with children of happy families. It is much more true where there is unhappiness. And unhappiness does not need to be obvious like drunkenness or violence. Grief not dealt with adequately, parents who push children to unrealistic achievements or who do not encourage children enough are just a few examples of the types of experience which affect people all through their life. Very often, counsellors will ask their clients about their childhood and be told that it was 'perfectly normal and happy'. But as the conversation goes on, unhappiness, which has long been buried, comes to the surface.

Research shows that people have an almost unerring instinct for 'choosing' another person who either 'matches' their unhappiness or 'makes up' for it.[4] This is unconscious. When we choose a partner, we only know that there is a 'chemistry' between us - that chemistry is composed of these unconscious factors. Counsellors call this 'marital fit'. When marriages get into difficulties, it is very often because one or more aspects of this 'fit' have altered. But because the couple did not understand the nature of the fit in the first place, they do not know what has gone wrong. They only experience that they are 'growing apart'. The Church has a part to play in helping couples to understand these unconscious factors better. For example, couples can be helped to 'tell their stories'. This is an essential part of the process a couple must go through before being accepted as adoptive parents - to 'tell their stories'. For the adoption agency, it is very revealing, but it is almost always so for the couple as well. They are helped to discover things they had hidden - unconsciously - from themselves and each other. People within the churches could be helped, with some basic training, to do this work with engaged couples.

Jack Dominion has spoken of the healing that goes on within marriage. We are all emotionally wounded in one way or another. But in marriage, we can be 'wounded healers' to each other, if we can understand one another's stories, and if we are able to be vulnerable to each other:

... wounds have important positive effects in creating a sense of community. The opening in the body is a channel of communication from one individual to another; the hazardous outflowing of blood an ultimate risking of the self for others ... but ... wounds, and the vulnerability which they represent, lead to healing only when they have been uncovered and dealt with; otherwise they are festering sores which destroy our health and the health of those with whom we deal.[5]

Alistair Campbell is speaking of giving pastoral care, but the same can be said of marriage where the partners may be pastors for each other. Telling our stories enables us to 'uncover the wounds' and is the beginning of the mutual healing process.

Telling our stories is the beginning of marriage preparation. Other work can be done, involving lay people in the churches as well as ministers, to help couples prepare for marriage. This is best done with groups of couples. Group preparation allows couples to learn from each other. A variety of methods can be used including role-plays, quizzes, games and discussion. A number of ready-made courses are available, some using video.[6]

It may be that marriage is too easy to begin. The church has a part to play in making it more difficult. Couples could be given much more help in discovering the reasons why they are wanting to be married. One possible exercise is to get couples to talk about the reasons other people have for marriage, and whether these are 'good' or 'bad' reasons. This gives them a chance to think about their own reasons. If this exercise is done with each couple by the same person who is involved in the 'story-telling', it can be very effective. Many couples marry for the wrong reasons; to gain status, to escape, etc. Many marry at the wrong time; when they are already coping with great stress because of, for example, pregnancy or bereavement. This is particularly so in second marriages. It is vital for the health of a new marriage that the 'old' one is finished, with issues of guilt and blame worked through, and problems relating to money, children etc. resolved. We have to be brave here and more ready to say to couples asking for marriage, 'Not yet'. This has to be done sensitively and from within the relationship we have formed with them.

Once a couple is married the church can help to support their marriage. This will be much easier if the relationship has been well made before the marriage. The couple will then see it as natural for the church to go on supporting and caring for them. Sensitive visits, especially during the most vulnerable first 12 months, cards on anniversaries, offers of baby-sitting, 'adopted grannies' within the congregation, especially when couples are away from their own parents can all provide great support. By having single-sex organisations (the 'women's meeting' or the 'men's group') the church often divides couples. There are plenty of activities for people separately - churches should be looking at forming groups for couples, with baby-sitting provided, where couples can be together.

There is also counselling. People need to be carefully selected, well trained and properly supported to do this work, but it is within the scope of churches to do much more than at present. Couples who have been supported in other ways by the church might find it a good deal easier to seek help within the church, and so might get help earlier, rather than wait till things have become almost intractable before going to an agency like Relate. Counselling depends on the honesty of the client. Jesus could only heal those who knew they needed to get better and wanted to do so. More than once, Jesus asked someone coming to him for healing: 'what do you want from me?' The counsellor often has to ask the client the same question.

Scripture and life experience tell us that it is in our interest as human beings to live in stable relationships. Marriage can be such a relationship. When the Church promotes healthy marriage it is promoting the health of individuals and of society as a whole. As in Jesus' time, so now, people sometimes make a mess of their relationships. This causes a great deal of pain. But here is the cross. Jesus accepted the pain of the cross in order to bring reconciliation. If the Church can learn to accept people, with their failings, their mess and their pain, then this is the beginning of healing and reconciliation.

This is a personal view of how churches might work *Towards Healthy Marriage*. It comes from my experience first as a minister, then as a Relate counsellor, and finally from what I have learned as a member of the Blackburn Marriage Education Group, an ecumenical group of clergy and lay people who seek to 'further thinking and action on the subject of marriage'. I would like to thank all the members of that group for their helpful comments on earlier drafts of this chapter.

1   C. Clulow and L. Cudmore *Marital Therapy, an inside view,* Tavistock Institute.
2   S. Kendall in the URC *Prayer Handbook,* URC, 1992, week 24.
3   URC *Service Book,* Oxford University Press, 1989, p.51.
4   An exercise which illustrates this is described in *Families and How to Survive Them*, by John Cleese and Robyn Skynner, published by Methuen. This is an excellent book about the factors which affect psychological development. The book is in the form of a conversation between the actor John Cleese and the psychologist and psychotherapist, Robyn Skynner. It has been made into a series on BBC Radio 4.
5   A. Campbell, *Rediscovering Pastoral Care,* Darton, Longman and Todd, 1981, pages 40-41.
6   Among many others, there are courses produced by the Church Pastoral Aid Society and Kensington Church Training. The Church of England group Family Life and Marriage Education (FLAME), which can be contacted through Church House, Deans Yard, Westminster, can provide details of different materials available. The author would be glad to provide details of the Blackburn Marriage Preparation course.

Divorce and remarriage

Bernard Thorogood

Jonathan: Here we are, please come in. Thank you for coming
to see me. We'll just get ourselves comfortable here in
the study. That's fine. You're Andrew and Clare and
you want me to take your wedding service in our
church. Fine, I'm glad you've come for a talk because
from what you said on the phone, Clare, I understand
that you both have been married before. So I have to
start out by letting you know that it is not an automatic
thing for me to take your wedding. In our church we
don't have to accept every couple. We think it is right
to enquire into the circumstances and get to know
people a little before we make a commitment, because
it is a very serious thing for me to lead you in the vows
and I don't do it lightly. So would you tell me
something of your stories. Let's start with you Andrew.

Andrew: It's not a story I enjoy telling, but of course I must
let you know how it happened with me. I was married
to Betty when I was twenty two and we were happy
together in a little terraced house in Manchester. The
service was in the local parish church, and my parents
came up from Plymouth and it was a great occasion.
I was working for British Rail then, away quite often.
Betty always gave me a great welcome when I got
home and it really felt like home. For four years there
was no sign of a baby coming though we both wanted
one very much. Then one day I got home and Betty
told me the news that she was pregnant, and we had a
celebration. It was just what we wanted. But a few
days later I took a phone call and a man's voice said,
"So glad Betty is pregnant, but ask her whose it is."
I couldn't believe it. And I couldn't ask her. But that
voice just kept repeating in my mind and in the end I
blurted it out. Betty looked deeply shocked but she just
stayed quiet. I pressed her for several days to deny that
story. Then she said, "I don't know whose it is." Well,
that knocked me over and gradually it came out that
she was actually slipping round to a neighbour when I

was away and that it was probably his baby. I couldn't stay there a day longer so I packed my bags and left. Within two years the divorce was started and Betty did not contest it. Now I've been living on my own for six years wondering if I would ever meet anyone else, and I know I've found the right person in Clare.

Jonathan: What a sad story. How lonely you must have been. But you didn't mention Betty's baby – did you ever see it?

Andrew: No. Once I'd left home I couldn't face it again, but of course I heard from friends and they all agreed that the baby was just like the neighbour, and as soon as the divorce was through Betty married him. So I'm quite sure it was not my child.

Jonathan: Perhaps you were rather quick to assume that. Perhaps you really wanted to escape.

Andrew: I don't know. It's hard to tell now. But I know we got married with every intention of keeping the vows and we were happy together and then it all went very wrong.

Jonathan: Now, Clare, perhaps you'd tell me a bit of your story.

Clare: My marriage to Adrian last ten years and we had no children. It all began as a friendship in the dramatic society attached to the United Reformed Church. We started going out together and everyone thought it was very suitable. We enjoyed each other's company. We almost drifted into marriage it seemed so easy. The service was in the church, and the minister was very encouraging. I suppose for four or five years we were good companions for each other. We went on with the dramatics and our holidays were fun. We were both in demanding jobs and did not really want children. But gradually the feeling between us began to change and the marriage began to seem more and more like a business arrangement. We worked long hours. Adrian would be exhausted when he got home. I would leave for work in the morning at 7.00am before he was awake. We only had time together at weekends and then I wanted to go to church and be with friends, while Adrian was all for driving miles to see business contacts or to examine new building projects. We reached the point of having two quite different lives in the same house, sharing nothing but the front door key. After a year or two of this I just couldn't stand it any more. It seemed like a nonsense marriage. We talked about it and agreed to separate for a while. I kept the house and Adrian moved to a flat in town. It really was a great release. I could relax. I could pick up all the local interests again. It felt good. So we came to an agreement that the separation and divorce should be made legal and really as I look back it seems as though that marriage never really took root in us at all. It was just a surface thing.

Jonathan: But when you felt it was going wrong didn't you try to do anything to save it?

Clare: Yes, but we weren't too concerned at the time. What seemed most important was the mortgage and our jobs and the hectic pace of life and inflation. We shared a bed and sometimes that was fun but sex didn't seem very important either, just a piece of icing on the cake. Looking back I can see that priorities were wrong but neither of us saw that at the time.

Jonathan: What has happened to Adrian? Do you ever hear from him?

Clare: Oh yes. We see each other sometimes and we can be quite friendly. There's no bad feeling. He has a girl friend, I think, but I don't enquire. He's getting high up in the quantity surveying business.

Jonathan: Thank you both for telling me that background. Let's have a cup of coffee before we go on.
        ... I'm sure you see why I asked you to tell me those stories of your lives. We are talking about the start of a marriage and the only honest way to approach that is to think what went wrong the first time. You come with very different experiences. You, Andrew, saw the failure of your marriage as being the unfaithfulness of

Betty, which you could not forgive. You did not say – and I'm not going to press you – whether you were always faithful to her. Yet in every marriage there are points of failure which we have to live with. For you this was a failure too great to accept and it destroyed in your heart the love you had. I can understand how that led to your divorce. It may have been the only route through an intolerable situation. But for you, Clare, the experience was very different. Your marriage seems to have been rather shaky from the start, almost as though it was something expected and pushed by all your friends, without any deep interest in each other as people. Then you drifted away from each other. But there must have been times when you could have stopped to think, put aside your diaries and looked at the needs of the other person. You accepted failure very easily and that makes me worried. What vision do you have of marriage to make it so important that you will try again?

Clare: I've learnt quite a lot. I know now that marriage is something to be worked at, not something that just falls into your lap with the wedding flowers. It's not a sideline for busy people. It does mean that loving includes taking time for each other.

Andrew: I think I've learned things too. There is a bit of unfaithfulness, a bit of wandering in our hearts and it's best to acknowledge that and face it rather than pretend we are perfect. I think humour is important so that we can laugh at ourselves – I never realised that before. Then there's a phrase I heard, perhaps it's from the Bible, about speaking the truth in love. I don't think I really did that with Betty. But Clare gives me such a sense of confidence that I believe that I could share everything with her.

Jonathan: You have both learnt important things. Those past events are serious; I don't gloss them over. You took marriage vows. You have not fulfilled them for a lifetime. But you know where things went wrong and now you want to start again. I believe that God always has room for people who want to start again, but only if

163

they have confessed their failure and tried to help anyone they have hurt. We take the vows 'till death us do part' and we can only take them if we truly mean them. But all of us are very imperfect people. We do make some wrong choices in our lives and I do not believe that a human vow can be so absolute that nothing can ever properly end it. There are moments when it is better to accept that we have made a mistake. Then at least there is a chance for doing better.

Andrew: You mean that just as the law recognises the end of a marriage, so the church can do so, and God can do so?

Jonathan: That's what I believe. Not every church says that and you know from your Anglican background that they may refuse to conduct your wedding. The Roman Catholic Church does not recognise divorce and remarriage at all. They see that as a basic defence of marriage as a life-long contract which may not be broken. I see their point of view but I do not share it. I think marriage is made for people, not people for marriage. If it is really for the good of the people to accept the breakdown then the church should accept it too. That is why I was so anxious to know what had happened to your first partners and whether you had dealt properly with them.

Clare: Does this mean that you will marry us in church? That's what we want to happen.

Jonathan: Yes, I'm ready to do that. We'll need to look at our diaries and see when it would be possible. But before we get to that let's think for a minute what that wedding service will mean. Both of you will need to start with the consciousness of the background. You, Andrew, will need to remember that Clare needs to be united with you at a far deeper level than ever happened with Adrian. You will need to talk with her about her work in the solicitor's office. You will think about her interests and get to know her friends. You will be with her in church on Sundays. You will plan good outings with her and enjoy music together. Do you think you can approach marriage with all that quite firm and clear?

Andrew: Yes. I have found already such a sense of closeness that all you have said is just putting into words what is already in my mind.

Jonathan: And you, Clare, can only approach this marriage knowing the great shock and loss that is behind Andrew. It may be he still needs reassurance that you will be faithful to him. He may have in his heart a dream of a child, and as you're both in your thirties there is no reason why you should not have a baby. You will have to put your heart into this marriage and your body too. Sex is not icing on the cake. It is about the depth of your love for each other and the commitment you are making. Can you come with that conviction?

Clare: That is exactly what is in my heart. I want to give Andrew the whole of myself. I'm thrilled that he cares for me so much.

Jonathan: There's another thing. Some of us have very traditional views about the roles of husband and wife. My guess is that you, Andrew, tend to picture your wife as a housewife while you, Clare, know that you are splendid in the office and perhaps not so much at home in the kitchen. You must be ready to meet the other person half way. I want you to talk about this to each other and be quite open about it. Will you do that?

Clare: Of course we must. Andrew, you don't mind me having a good job do you?

Andrew: No, I'm proud of that. But I hope that if a baby comes along you will not think it is somehow a let-down to stay at home.

Clare: Hardly that. A baby would be such a tremendous event it would probably shake both of us and change our ideas. But I hope you would wash the nappies too.

Andrew: I'm not saying that's my life ambition. But yes, we must share just as much as we can. And I do very much hope for a baby.

Jonathan: must keep thinking along those lines. Now before we finish this and look at dates let us imagine we are in the church and you are just about to make the vows. You are going to say in the presence of God and of the congregation of friends that you will be faithful to each other for the rest of your lives. We know that human mistakes happen. But I can only ask you to make that promise if it is with your whole heart, your whole intention, your total commitment. And I can only do this in church if you believe that we are God's children in his world and that he has made us to care for one another. Do you see what I mean? You can always go to the Registrar's office if the marriage is just a contract between the two of you. But you have asked to be in the church and I'm so glad about that. I just don't want you to misunderstand. You will make promises which are very serious and you will pray that God will help you to keep them.

Clare: Thank you. That is exactly how I feel about it. I can't imagine any better way of starting our life together.

Andrew: Yes, it is the moment of hope and joy. And we mean to keep it that way.

Jonathan: Let's go into the church ...

Jonathan: God, you make it easy for some people and hard for me. If there were just one total rule then I could turn them away with a good conscience. But I can't do that. We have to judge whether it is a proper moment to be generous or a moment to be strict. We have to look whether they are being flippant or sincere. And we make mistakes sometimes. But I thought I saw love there, not a springtime fanciful love but a mature and thoughtful love. So I said 'yes'. Lord, it is very hard for us to know whether this is just being soft-hearted and in tune with the times or whether it is truly your way of forgiveness and renewal. Could it be something of both? Could you be teaching us that divorce is not just sin and not just weakness but a way of coming to terms with our humanity? Yet that does not satisfy me either. You seek to lift our humanity and purify it and fill it with your Spirit. So do you seek to keep our standards high and expect the very best and urge people to stay together?

Yes, Lord, help me always to expect the best and encourage the best. May we in this church extend a hand to all who struggle through rough places in marriage. But when it collapses and when the real bond of heart and mind and body is broken, then let us not be too legalistic but still seek the best, the best for those who are separated, the best for any children, the best for the future. May we find new beginnings, Lord of healing and hope. Amen.

Separation and divorce

Jean Mortimer

Although the case study with which this chapter begins is written in the third person it is an account of my own experience. I have chosen to present it in this way to try to give greater objectivity to what is of necessity a highly personal and one-sided account and in the hope that this format may be useful for discussion purposes. My former husband and my sons are aware of what I have written.

Case Notes

Husband: (42) successful executive in a multi-national company, member of the United Reformed Church and a serving elder in his local congregation.

Wife: (44) a minister of the United Reformed Church recently returned to full-time pastoral charge in the same local congregation after several years of part-time ministry while their sons were growing up.

Children: two teenage sons, the elder (16) living at home and preparing for GCSE examinations, the younger (14) away from home at a residential school for children with emotional and learning difficulties.

After six months in her pastorate the wife had major spinal surgery, a degenerative condition was diagnosed and she was advised to resign from full-time ministry. In the midst of her double bereavement her husband was under great stress at work, his mother was dying and their sons were adjusting to adolescence and the family's removal to a new area following the husband's promotion. Soon after his mother's death the husband left the family home, established himself in a flat nearby and declared his intention of seeking a divorce. After several discussions he agreed to a Deed of Separation on condition that if, after two years, either party wished to re-marry, a petition for divorce would not be contested. For the wife and sons, who did not want the marriage to end, this decision gave some grounds for hope that as there appeared to be no other person involved, such a breathing space might help towards some kind of reconciliation.

Soon afterwards the wife's health deteriorated even further and a second, more extensive spinal operation was carried out. During her convalescence it became clear that the husband was forming a relationship with someone else. In due course the husband petitioned for divorce on the grounds of two years separation and the wife felt bound by the terms of their separation not to contest this. Shortly after the decree absolute was granted, her former husband announced his intention of re-marrying in the church where she had formerly ministered and where he had continued to serve as an elder. The minister who had succeeded her agreed to this request without consulting the elders or church meeting, a practice which had always been observed in all previous ministries, even though the new partner had previously been married and divorced several times and was neither a member nor adherent of the church. This break with the previously accepted pastoral practice of the church caused a great deal of anxiety and distress for several of the elders and for the wife when some of these elders contacted her to discuss their difficulties.

Although colleagues and friends offered a great deal of patient listening, support and prayer throughout this painful time she received only one visit from her moderator which was at her own request. He neither prayed with her nor offered to discuss any of her emotional and spiritual problems. The majority of his remarks were related to matters of a financial and administrative nature. At this point in the proceedings it became a matter of emotional, spiritual and theological urgency for the wife to be released from her marriage vows. In the absence of any officially agreed liturgy for such a purpose she invited the minister who had conducted their marriage service to discuss with her some of her unresolved questions and to prepare a suitable service of release. Her former husband declined her invitation to take part in this and, in the light of his response, she decided that it would not be helpful to ask their sons to be present. Had his response been more positive she would have suggested that the liturgy be used as a means of shared acceptance and forgiveness and as a way of reconciling everyone to the new family situation. In the event, she was left with a rather one-sided feeling about the whole experience but it did help to resolve some of her problems and was the best that could be done in the circumstances. It was also the starting point for some of the reflections which follow.

Personal Reflections

On the face of it this looks like a story of desertion, dishonesty, rejection, adultery and inadequate pastoral support on a grand scale, and that is exactly how it felt to me at the time. I, who had stood by him, helped him, moved around the country for the sake of his career at the expense of fulfilment in my own, was being deserted when I most needed his love and support. They, our children, at the very time when it was important in their development to have a close bond with their male parent, were losing their father and their confidence in those appointed by the church to act as 'Father in God' to their mother and to them. I, who had made excuses for his behaviour, both publicly and privately to avoid compromising his position as an elder of the church and to safeguard his relationship with our sons was made to feel a liar and a fool when it became apparent that his intentions in respect of his later relationship had been forming at the time when he first left us. I, who through all the difficult and painful period of our separation had tried to maintain some semblance of family life in the midst of my own emotional and physical pain, loving and supporting our children and bearing the added burden of the grief and distress of my former congregation, now felt both personally and professionally abandoned. I, who had never been unfaithful to him in nearly twenty years of a marriage which had been unfulfilling in a variety of ways had been cast aside for a younger, fitter and more attractive woman. Despite the love and support of those already mentioned in the case notes, I felt a complete failure as a woman, a wife and a minister and sank into a deep depression which brought me to the brink of suicide.

What a tale of woe!

Writing about it in this way brings back much of the pain I felt at that time and the knowledge that there are many others who have gone through similar and even more distressing experiences without adequate support and understanding from the Church makes these recollections all the more poignant. I do not, however, regret my decision to write in this way, for this, more than anything else, has helped me to see that such wounds can be healed. It is my earnest hope that what I have written may be of some help to such people.

Five years on from that painful time I am now able to see things in a very different light. The most appropriate word to describe this new perspective is LIBERATION. I write it in such bold letters because that is how it feels today and I am confident that I will continue to feel that same sense of liberation in the days which lie ahead. BUT, it has been achieved at a price which I consider to have been unduly high, not only for myself, but also for my former husband, my sons, my family and friends and not least my former congregation.

Had my husband not found the courage to be the one to take the risk of public censure, by leaving a marriage which had been broken and empty for a number of years, I am fairly certain that I would have gritted my teeth and persevered with it; partly because of my position as an ordained minister, partly out of fear of facing increasing pain and disability alone and partly because of cultural and religious conditioning that this is 'what being a good Christian wife, mother and minister' requires. Such perseverance would have reinforced my sense of 'martyrdom' for the sake of being seen to be doing the right thing but I do not consider that it would have been healthy for any of us within the family. Nor do I believe that the Church has any right to expect such costly perfection from its members or professional representatives. In such circumstances it can therefore be argued that it is a braver, more genuinely Christian act to go rather than to stay. So how can such a leaving be counted as 'desertion'? The adversarial nature of much of the legal proceedings prior to divorce or separation does nothing to prevent the formulation of such partial judgements. Furthermore, although my former husband was not able to be entirely open about his already half-formed intentions with regard to a new relationship, I can now see that this may in part have been his way of trying to avoid some of the harmful gossip which might have made our respective positions in the church untenable. I also see that I was no less dishonest in maintaining the public pretence that all was well between us when in fact it had not been so for some time. Perhaps in this respect we each became the victims of what we thought would be expected of us by the Church? If his decision to leave did indeed make me feel totally rejected, how often had he been made to feel the same by my pastoral involvement with others at his or our sons' expense? Was his physical involvement with someone else after the separation any more adulterous in terms of biblical teaching than the 'adultery in the heart' to which I had succumbed at a particularly difficult period in our marriage? It was not easy to raise such questions with myself and to face up to the implications of trying to give honest answers. I was enabled to do so by a wise and patient professional counsellor whom I saw, at my own expense, for over a year. It would have been easier if such ministry had been offered to me from within the Church. I do not know if my former husband felt the same but I suspect that he too would have appreciated the offer of such help.

These reflections highlight the inadequacy of the current situation with regard to support for couples whose marriages are under stress, both within the church and in the secular sphere, especially in situations like my own, where one partner is reluctant for the marriage to end so abruptly. They also raise questions about the responsibility of the Church to find acceptable and appropriate ways of providing support and advice to ministers and their spouses, families and congregations when there are marriage difficulties. It is not enough to leave this to chance in the rather ad hoc way which is currently the case in many instances. I am deeply grateful to all who, at my request, listened and helped me to unravel some of the issues which concerned me most at this time, and particularly thankful to my colleague and friend, the Reverend Norman Charlton, who prepared my liturgy of release and to his wife, Vera, who shared in it with us. This was the real turning point from which my feelings of liberation began to grow. They have become stronger with time as I have found the courage to be and to minister in new ways and as friends have offered a ministry of affirmation by pointing me along these previously untried ways. The request to write this chapter represents one such example. Those who have invited me to conduct their marriage services have probably not realised how much this has meant to me. It feels good to be able to take this opportunity of expressing my thanks for this support and encouragement. I hope that the ministry I have offered to them has been deeper and more meaningful because of my own experience of having come through the pain, guilt, forgiveness and renewal associated with the failure of my own marriage.

Questions and Answers

The most pressing reason for the urgency which I felt about being released from my marriage vows was related to the Church's understanding of the nature of a vow or sacred promise. The preamble to a Christian marriage service implies that this commitment is not something to be undertaken lightly or carelessly with the attitude that if it does not work out it can be set aside by the decision of a divorce court. The promises in a secular marriage ceremony also stress a lifelong commitment. I had made such a commitment to my husband before God and regarded God as a vital third party to it. To honour my husband's decision to set aside his part of that commitment I was being placed in a position of having to break a solemn promise to God and felt a deep need to be assured that God would understand this predicament and forgive me for my part in the circumstances which had caused it. In my own ministry I had always taken great care to stress the importance of this aspect of the marriage service when preparing others to make their commitment, so there was a double sense of guilt about being seen to have failed to take it seriously in my own life. It was impossible to minister to myself in this situation, hence my deep disappointment and anger that such ministry was not offered by the official representative of the Church.

The second question which troubled me concerned the lack of any officially agreed guidelines for ministers and local churches in terms of how they should respond to requests for re-marriage especially where, as in my own case, one of the partners had previously been married and divorced and was not associated with the Church in any way. It was clear to me, that, had there been such guidelines some of the distress felt by members of my former congregation might have been avoided. This aspect of the case highlights a more fundamental theological question concerning the law/gospel paradigm. How can a Church which sanctions the re-marriage of divorced people establish an appropriate balance between law and gospel, judgement and love in maintaining lifelong marriage as the ideal state, whilst at the same time offering forgiveness and the chance to make a fresh start to those who have failed, once or more than once, to live up to this ideal? Is more careful marriage preparation an important part of the answer? Should ministers be advised to give stronger direction towards a civil ceremony to couples who have reservations about making such a lifelong commitment before God both in the first instance or in the case of requests for re-marriage? Is an officially agreed liturgy of release a tacit admission that the expectation of lifelong commitment is too high for some people? Is it a dangerous form of casuistry to suggest some form of compromise whereby couples who genuinely seek the support and blessing of the Church and who prefer a legal marriage to a common law arrangement, but who, for whatever reasons do not feel able to make the lifelong commitment currently required by both Church and state, might be offered a less demanding form of words for first or subsequent marriages? All of these are very big questions to which there are

no easy answers, but in the light of the general divorce statistics
and the high incidence of ministerial marriage problems they
cannot be fudged or ignored.

Six months after my own liturgy of release I took part in a
consultation on divorce and separation organised by The United
Reformed Church in the United Kingdom at its Windermere
Centre. During that consultation several of the questions raised in
this chapter were discussed and although there was a wide variety
of opinion as to how the Church might begin to formulate answers,
there was general agreement that not enough is being done. Since
then, two similar consultations have been held, one of which has
dealt with the subject of the failure of ministerial marriages. My
own tentative attempts to suggest answers may not suffice for
everyone and I recognise that there are no pious placebos to take
away the pain of such experiences. But I am convinced that it is
only as the Church begins to wrestle with such problems that it
will begin to find a way forward and maintain any real credibility
in our rapidly changing society, where some of the traditional
expectations of marriage, family life, the role of women, the role of
the minister and the role of the Church are being called in question.
I have no wish to compromise the Church's teaching on marriage
or its expectations of the standard of public and private morality of
its members and ministers to the point at which they cease to have
any impact or meaning. But neither do I want to see people paying
mere lip service to impossible demands which they know they
cannot fulfil. For these reasons, I do not think that it would be
inappropriate for the Church to offer different forms of liturgy for
marriage, so as to respond to the needs of those who wish to make
a lifelong commitment before God and those who in conscience
cannot express their commitment in such absolute terms. Nor do I
think that an officially agreed order for a service of release from
either form of commitment would erode the Church's influence and
ideals. If the love and forgiveness of God for all people is to have
any meaning, then the Church needs to move away from a theology
of strength and success towards a theology of weakness and failure
recognising that it is not a simple case of either/or but a far more
complex situation in which the apparently contradictory nature of
such false polarities can be challenged in the interest of developing
a more holistic approach to doctrine, liturgy and pastoral care. In
preparing couples and, where appropriate, whole families for such
services, ministers would be required to offer a deeper level of
counselling and support. This would have serious implications for

theological training and post-ordination guidance, training and professional supervision. It would also raise further questions about the ministry of all God's people and might lead to a deeper theology of ministry and a more sensitive understanding of the pressure under which many ministers work as a result of their own and other people's unrealistic expectations of their role. Above all, it might lead the whole Church to the point at which together we are able to accept that it is within our honest strivings to face up to the painful and difficult consequences of asking such questions that we will encounter anew the God, who, in Christ has promised to be with us and at one with us in all our celebration, strength and success and in our separation, sorrow and sin. Though we in our fickleness and ever-present frailty may continue to bend or break our human promises, God's covenant of loving judgement never fails.

Broken But Not Beyond Repair

Promises broken
Trust betrayed
Bitter words spoken
Tempers frayed
Empty loneliness
Darkness and pain
Children's distress
Cries to God – in vain?
Hearts and lives broken
Love raw and flayed
Future uncertain
Costs to be paid
BUT WE ARE STILL CHRIST'S BODY
His tears and cross our token
That God's loving judgement aches to fulfil
All that our striving to love has broken.

(Windermere Centre, Spring 1992, with love and thanks to all who were there.)

Words of Jesus which may help you

John Taylor

There can be few families that are unaffected by the crisis in
marriage and sexual relationships today. Few of us have not shared
the distress of daughters and sons, friends and workmates when
their lives have been devastated by broken relationships. We may
have experienced it personally. It is a crisis troubling society as a
whole, all walks of life. Recently a bank manager, shaking his
head, said, 'Half my time is spent counselling clients and staff over
domestic troubles, not money matters, and I've never been trained
for it'. But above all it is the plight of children from broken homes,
growing up with divided loyalties, which saddens and worries us
most. Some of them get badly spoiled by jealous parents. Others
are neglected. Others feel second-class living alongside half-
brothers and sisters of a second and successful marriage.

Can we find any help in scripture? What about *Mark 10:2-12*?
Here Jesus' constant critics are trying to confound him over divorce.
Would he go as far as to defy Moses who allowed it? Jesus was
astute and did not attack the law of Moses head on but he came
close to it.

'But Jesus said to them, 'Because of your hardness of heart he wrote
this commandment for you. But from the beginning of creation,
'God made them male and female'. 'For this reason a man shall
leave his father and mother and be joined to his wife, and the two
shall become one flesh'. Then he concluded with words which are
quoted at our marriage services, 'Therefore what God has joined
together, let no one separate.'

Some people feel that marriage is on the way out. I do not think
so. Why? For the reason Jesus gives. The genesis of marriage is
the need of male and female for each other. Thus God made us.
My view is that fundamentally marriage is the union of male and
female. The ceremonies we have to celebrate this serve to regulate
private love. The ancient law was that if consummation did not
take place then the legal ties became null and void. Marriage
customs have varied from place to place and age to age and I
expect the next century will have to make changes to embrace and
sustain the social order, but I would be most surprised if men and
women ceased to want loving, long-lasting unions.

'Because of your hardness of heart', said Jesus, Moses permitted divorce. This is readily understandable when we visualise what used to happen in those days. A man, middle-aged, comfortably off, with grown-up children, would become enamoured of a girl and decide to discard his wife. So long as he made adequate provision for her, he could divorce her. It was plainly hardhearted. No doubt, Jesus was expressing what most women felt, and decent men.

Is not hardness of heart the root-cause of our troubles? To insist on getting your own way, to brush aside your partner's needs and feelings, to assume you are right and the other wrong, to fail to share burdens, to walk out at will, and so on - isn't it to manifest hardness of heart? Yet none of this should seem surprising to us in an age which has cultivated the individual's freedom at the expense of responsibilities, rights rather than duties, and has idolised self-fulfilment, despising self-denial. Breakdown in marriage is but a part of the general decline of moral standards.

The Greek word for hardness of heart is *sklerokardia* - sclerosis of the heart! Vivid indeed, yet if you look at some modern versions you get a shock. In the *New English Bible* we find it rendered, 'having your minds closed' and in the *Good News Bible* 'you are so hard to teach'. The explanation is that in Hebrew thinking the heart was not considered the centre of the emotions so much as of reason, will and attitude. Most people were open to reason, but some were stubborn.

It is precisely in this area, the area of character building, that we have seen neglect and we need revival. Tycoons and stars of different kinds have been our models. Christ has been ignored. For a better society we need good models. I was brought up in a school with high standards in academic work and sport, but we were never left in any doubt that what mattered most was a good, reliable, gentle, kind and strong character. I am glad I was thus trained and avoided *sklerocardia*! I hope that kind of character training may bloom afresh.

Lastly, a word about the next few verses which form an appendix to the story. We learn that subsequently, in private, the disciples began questioning Jesus and he made two further points. Firstly, that anyone divorcing a wife and remarrying would be committing adultery, and secondly, that this applied equally to women who divorced husbands. This is fascinating because whereas in Jewish law men only had access to divorce, in Roman law women had the right too. And if you turn to Matthew's version you find that a man may seek divorce if his wife has been adulterous. My view is that in these verses what we see is the early Church filling out Jesus' rather basic teaching to meet the needs of Jews and Gentiles. Unfortunately the Church has often made these rules into cast-iron laws which people would have to be ideal to keep. It seems inconceivable that someone whose marriage has broken and vanished is condemned to an impossible celibacy or a sinful liaison registered as a marriage by the state. Doesn't grace, doesn't forgiveness exist where marriage is concerned? I am glad to have married many divorced people and moreover, to be able to testify to their lasting happiness in many, many cases.

I find Mark's Gospel a great help in wrestling with the marriage crisis. It points me in certain directions. Of course it does not solve our problems for us. That is something we all have to do slowly and painfully, I fear. I trust that our saving God will lead us to better times. I hope you share my overall confidence.

On the death of a spouse

Margaret Nuttall

It all began one summer evening in Scotland where we were on holiday. My husband had been in Canada giving a course of lectures and was joining us for the rest of the holiday before the start of the autumn term. When we met him at the station I thought he looked thin and tired, but a week of east coast air and the joy of being together again soon restored him to his usual vigour. One evening after tea the two of us set off along the shore to walk to the harbour when I noticed he was stumbling in the heavy sand. When we returned home he said he had no sensation in his right hand and foot, and he couldn't write - signs of a mild stroke which neither of us recognised. It was the beginning of an illness now known as Alzheimer's, and which was to reduce him both physically and mentally until he could no longer walk, and finally hardly knew us. He died ten years later, and the effects of his slow decline on myself and the family were cataclysmic - a long process of grieving that turned our life upside down. The girls were ten, thirteen and sixteen years old when it started, and each has been profoundly affected - losing a father who had read stories to them, taken them walking, played the piano, and just always was there: losing him while he was still alive.

The Abyss

I have learned that bereavement takes many forms and the experience of each person is unique. For us it happened over a period of time when my husband was still alive yet hardly with us. It was a time of incredible stress - of ignorance of the cause or even the name of the illness, of frustration at the lack of communication with someone who had been so vital and gifted, and of increasing isolation from friends and colleagues. Most of them couldn't understand and couldn't cope with what was happening to someone they knew so well. He was unable to discuss how he felt, unable to take any decisions, and I had to write his letter of resignation for him. All the things he valued seemed to be taken from him - his work, his music (he was a good pianist), his country walks, his reading, even his friends.

I recently saw a drawing by a cancer patient showing a large dragon eating flowers at the feet of a small child. The dragon represented her illness and she was the child. The flowers were the precious things she was losing. It reminded me of how his illness devoured all the things that Harry enjoyed and valued, and all that he was. It wasn't only his talents that were swallowed up but he himself seemed to shrivel. He once in the early days said to me, 'Don't forget that I'm the same person,' yet it was hard to accept changes in his behaviour, his restless vagueness, his gradual loss of mental faculties which prevented communication between us, and the awful knowledge that things would surely get worse. In my mind's eye I could see the wheel chair before he actually needed one.

We shared an interest in theology, but his illness deprived us of any conversation. I came to know the feeling of the abyss described by Kierkegaard, but was not aware of meeting God there - only perplexity and anguish. There was no one with whom to share the blankness and I came to realise how appropriate is the term broken-hearted. Grief is physical in its manifestation - just as if a flat sword is plunged into the heart and periodically turned. The combination of ignorance, helplessness and terror in the midst of ordinary daily life with its semblance of normality is a feature of bereavement that can tip one over the edge to doubt one's own sanity. There's no escape from the enormity of what's happening, no solution to the questioning, no release from the tension and despair. Among the notes and jottings that I kept in those years are the lines from *King Lear:*

O the mind has mountains, cliffs of fall
frightful, sheer, no-man fathomed.
Hold them cheap may who ne'er hung there.

Although mind and spirit are at stretch God is absent. It is a time of dereliction and forsakenness in which one can identify with Jesus' cry from the cross, 'My God, my God why have you forsaken me?' The question 'Why?' is at the heart of the Lord's suffering as it is of our own, and it is the point where we find our identity with him, for no answer comes for him either. I think the answer is in the question itself, for how can we cry out if we do not in some way believe that someone is there to hear?

The Loss of Identity

> He who binds unto himself a joy
> Doth the winged life destroy;
> But he who kisses the joy as it flies
> Dwells in Eternity's sunrise.[1]

These words by Blake seemed to underscore our original relationship, and we both realised from the beginning of our life together that love requires freedom. Yet I was unprepared for the feeling of desolation and loneliness that came with his slow decline and loss. I no longer knew who I was, for my identity was linked to his. It was embarrassing to meet people who didn't know what to say to me, and just as difficult to find words to answer their questions. I was cut off from the social life we used to enjoy together, and the few friends who came to the house had to be warned not to stay long. My mind was pre-occupied and I remember standing absent-mindedly in the greengrocer's one day and being asked rather sharply by the assistant, 'Do you want this rhubarb or not?'!

I found myself noticing couples and being jealous of their happy relationship - feeling excluded from normal companionship and deprived of personal affection. I know now that these feelings are common in bereavement. They sap confidence and add to one's isolation and perplexity. The loss of intimacy and close support of a partner contribute to a sense of unworthiness and dereliction, and nothing seems to be important any more. There is a great weight of unhappiness which affects the whole family. With hindsight I could have been more supportive of the girls, and could perhaps have confided in them and so shared the burden - but my problems were not theirs, and there was an over-riding practical need to maintain the home. I know better now, but it was not obvious at the time.

The Re-discovery of Self

A patient who had been widowed said to me recently, 'It's not true that time heals. I grieve for my husband now just as much as I did when he died.' I think this may be true, since part of oneself is also lost, but somehow this later grief has a different focus. There is more distance and objectivity about it. I do not speak of endless pathological grieving which is an affliction needing treatment. It is normal to feel sad at times. Familiar passages of piano music still awaken memories - Brahms' Intermezzo and the Rhapsody catch one unawares when heard unexpectedly on the radio, but the sadness is less devastating. Soon after Harry died a friend who knew us both said, 'I think you're getting round a very long corner.' I felt that this was true, and the fact that it took so long to happen meant that much of the work of grieving had already been done. I can identify the time when re-building began, though it was with great reluctance that I let him go. Letting go means acknowledging the reality of loss and looking to a new personal future. It began when I realised that I had no longer a husband but rather a patient with needs and total dependence. Once that is accepted the frustration becomes less. It's not easy to accept because one has needs of one's own that are not being met - but in the end it's better to recognise it than to go on being resentful. It may be necessary for an outsider to give one permission to let go, and in this case it was my father who simply told me I couldn't go on giving the same degree of physical care. The advice was therapeutic, and as his life in hospital was ending - without speech or recognition - I began to consider how I might spend the time ahead, when I would be on my own.

A friend recently bereaved said that she felt very selfish with only herself to look after, and I think one can be swept by feelings of guilt after a life-time of caring for husband and family. One can also feel guilty at the relief when the long strain is over. In spite of a great mixture of feelings I became aware that I was being picked up and my life was being given a new direction. I could look to the future knowing there was healing to be had, and even happiness.

In his book on Christian spirituality The wound of knowledge, Rowan Williams identifies the action of God in human life as seen by Augustine: 'A human life is given its unity and its intelligibility from outside: when God pulls taut the slack thread of desire, binding it to Himself, the muddled and painful litter of experience is gathered together and given direction.'[2]

The Unexpected Bonus

Recovery from the loss of a marriage partner is a hard reminder that healing isn't achieved by one's own efforts but is a gift. One also learns that the path to deeper understanding of God leads through the middle of suffering. This hard fact lies at the heart of the dying and rising of Christ and at the heart of our human experience of loss and recovery. Death and resurrection not only take place at the end of life here, but occur throughout in the troubles and triumphs which come our way. There is mystery in the contradiction of finding life through death, and seeing failure as a gateway to hope.

> Two trees
> proclaim in spring
> a word to the world
>
> one exploding
> into blossom
> trumpets its glory
>
> one stretching
> dead limbs
> holds the empty
> body of God
>
> both speak
> with due reserve
> into the listening
> ear of the world. [3]

Maria Boulding quotes this verse by Ralph Wright in her book Gateway to hope. It represents the loss and gain built into the human enterprise as the way of leading us to God. It is a matter of observation, not of moral judgement, that God can bring life out of death, good out of evil and hope out of despair.

In *When Bad Things Happen to Good People*,[4] Rabbi Harold Kushner describes the slow deterioration of his son and his early death from a wasting disease. There is, he says, no way that he would have wished this to happen - yet he realises now that he is a better rabbi because of it. It has not been total disaster.

This is the unexpected bonus - an insight into other people's suffering which enables us to be alongside and available at a point of need. Henri Nouwen calls such a companion the wounded healer.[5] He offers this as a model to those in pastoral care, indeed to anyone in a helping role which so often can be patronising. The wounded healer recognises his or her own weakness and vulnerability, and shares the helplessness of the sufferer, creating a bond of understanding within the silence of God.

1 W. Blake, *Eternity.* The Faber Book of Religious Verse, 1972, p.232.
2 R. Williams, *The Wound of Knowledge,* Darton Longman & Todd, 1979, p.82.
3 M. Boulding, *Gateway to Hope,* Fount, 1985, p.72.
4 H. Kushner, *When Bad Things Happen to Good People,* Pan, 1982.
5 H. Nouwen, *The Wounded Healer,* Image, 1979.

Prayer

May the God who made us for one another,
who loves us with a faithful love
and whose Spirit makes us passionate and strong,
bless us and embrace us,
now and forever. Amen.

(Susan Durber)

Recommended reading

D. Atkinson *To have and to hold: The marriage covenant and the discipline of divorce,* Collins, 1979.

J. Bagot *How to Understand Marriage,* SCM, 1987.

J. Dominion *Marriage, Faith and Love,* Darton, Longman and Todd, 1981.

S. Dowell *They Two Shall Be One. Monogamy in history and religion,* Collins, 1990.

M. Furlong *Mirror to the Church; reflections on sexism,* SPCK, 1988.

H. Oppenheimer *Marriage,* Mowbray, 1990.

E. Schillebeeckx *Marriage; Secular Reality and Saving Mystery* (Two volumes), Sheed and Ward, 1965.

E. Stuart *Daring to Speak Love's Name,* Hamish Hamilton, 1993.

P. Trible *God and the Rhetoric of Sexuality,* SCM, 1978.

J. Zizoulas *Being as Communion,* St Valdimir's Seminary Press, 1985.

Permission has been sought for the use of extracts from:

The New Jerusalem Bible
published by Darton Longman and Todd

Towards Healthy Marriage (Pete Rand)
published by Darton Longman and Todd

Testament of Youth (Vera Britten)
Published by Virago

Marriage for Love (Strauss)
published by Tyndale House